REBEL
EDUCATOR

REBEL
EDUCATOR

Create Classrooms Where
IMPACT and IMAGINATION Meet

Tanya Sheckley

HOUNDSTOOTH
PRESS

REBEL EDUCATOR
Create Classrooms Where Impact and Imagination Meet

ISBN   978-1-5445-2980-6   *Hardcover*
        978-1-5445-2981-3   *Paperback*
        978-1-5445-2982-0   *Ebook*
        978-1-5445-3094-9   *Audiobook*

CONTENTS

INTRODUCTION

A Rebel Educator understands the driving forces behind education and sees a better way. They resist tradition in teaching, seek innovation, and are constantly learning.

Rebel Educators understand the importance of engaging curriculum that has real purpose. They don't teach because they want their students to get good scores—they want their students to be good people. Rebel Educators seek to become more than granters of knowledge and wish to draw out the light in every student. They engineer learning experiences and facilitate student growth.

Regardless of how long you have been teaching or what constraints you have on your lessons and ideas, it's never too late to become a Rebel Educator. In this book, you will encounter stories and quotes from educators, writers, thought leaders, and students that will inspire your teaching, rekindle your joy in the classroom, and provide context for challenges in the educational system. Whether you teach in a classroom or a forest, a commercial building or a home, you will find methods to enhance your craft. It will encourage you to embrace a project-based and student-aligned philosophy of teaching. I hope it will help you begin, or continue, to build inquiry and experience in your classroom.

The ideas inside *Rebel Educator* will help you build classroom relationships, ignite creativity, nurture curiosity, and turn your classrooms into places of wonder. Your students will love coming to school and, more importantly, so will you.

When we start making changes and working together toward a goal, we can make real change within our educational system. This book is for teachers starting out and searching for ideas. It's for seasoned teachers looking to shift the culture of their classroom, and it's for school leaders who want to create better learning environments and experiences to support the emotional and academic needs of their students and teachers. Really, it's for anyone who works with children.

This book discusses project-based learning and experiential learning; I will often use these terms interchangeably, although there are subtle differences. A project is a multi-subject collaboration that works on understanding a concept through seeking solutions to a driving question. It may include research elements, knowledge-building elements, activities, experiences, and deliverables. It is a series of events, experiences, and lessons designed to offer the student a pathway to solutions while creating open-ended questions to explore areas of interest within the concept and theme.

Experiential learning encompasses each experience we create for our students throughout their learning. Each time they experience something new, whether it is creating, building, listening to an expert, taking a field trip, or presenting their learning, they are experiencing learning in action—experiential learning. Project-based learning is inherently experiential. There are many experiences within a project, but experiential learning can take place in any subject on any day at any point in learning. Experiencing our learning helps us to learn and remember better.

The information you will find in this book isn't particularly new, but it is put together in new ways. This is not a deep dive into any one theory of learning—inquiry, project, concept, forest, Montessori, Reggio, personalized, differentiated, among others. Rather, it works to tie many of these together in the best possible ways. That is what we have done with our school, UP Academy, and it is what I challenge you to do in your classrooms. Create your own method. Build your own curriculum. Find ways to bring joy to the classroom and support students in making a difference in the world around them.

THE AUTHOR'S STORY

I never liked kids. It wasn't until I was in my thirties and my best friend had a daughter that I changed my mind. One day, this little girl was learning to walk; three weeks later she was problem solving how to run around her mom's legs to reach the toy she wanted. Seeing how quickly and joyfully she learned finally convinced me that kids were alright.

I didn't intend to start a school. I got an MBA in Entrepreneurship with the intent of starting a business, not a school. I spent almost a decade in sales and marketing, selling beer. But after having three children, all with different needs, and not finding a school that could include and support all of them, I saw an opportunity.

I could build something new and different that would support the needs of my children and so many others that had been forgotten, left behind, passed over, or put in the wrong classroom.

My oldest daughter, Eliza, was born with cerebral palsy. She was bright, observant, and social, but needed extra support to gain independence and to be successful in her academics. Our school tried its best, but she wasn't getting the therapeutics or academics she needed to successfully navigate the world. I talked to other parents and realized many had the same frustrations I did. I could see another way and decided to work towards starting a school.

Within six months, we had articles of incorporation, bylaws, and a board of directors. We received 501(c)(3) status in December 2015, and I started actively searching for locations for the school. Then we had an unexpected tragedy—at only six years old, Eliza passed away. Our family did a lot of soul searching and decided we had learned so much from Eliza that we wanted to share it with other families and make a difference in the lives of other children. We sought to find purpose in our grief. We believed that Eliza taught us how to be kind, strong, and to always do our best. We continue to hold these values in the school and in our family.

We believed that by including students of different abilities in the same classes, all students could thrive. This approach would build social and emotional skills, empathy, and creativity, and create a generation that saw all people as capable. It would give students who hadn't been given a chance a new one, and students who had been passed over, more attention. This huge project has taught me more than I ever expected and given me more meaning and joy in my life. But this book is not only about inclusive education; it is also about shifting our classrooms to respect and honor the intelligence and capability of all students. It focuses on creating experiences, building projects, inviting community involvement, and creating safe spaces for creativity, collaboration, and growth.

We created UP Academy to give every student the opportunity to reach their Ultimate Potential. This is where the UP in UP Academy comes from. We chose to open an independent school free of the bureaucracy, policies, and procedures that make change difficult in large structured organizations—a school where we could mold and create a new method of education that we could share to support countless children around the world. This book is the beginning.

I share my story because I wasn't trained as an educator. I learned what I know about education through doing, seeing, and replicating other educators I met and respected. This gives me the perspective to disrupt education as I see it—to be a Rebel Educator.

In addition to the many experiences, discussions, and interviews I conducted for this book, I also rely on the work of Barry G. Sheckley, Ray Neag Professor of Education, Emeritus at the University of Connecticut, and recipient of national awards recognizing his research on how students learn best. I read "What to Do with Reclaimed Instructional Time," which summarizes, with specific examples from classroom applications, how teachers can structure experiences that foster students' learning by enhancing their agency as learners.[1] As I wrote this book, I used examples from this summary chapter to support key ideas. (Full disclosure: Barry is also a helpful father-in-law who served as a valuable resource to me as I developed the ideas outlined in this book.) He has given me and UP Academy countless hours to help us shape

---

1   Barry G. Sheckley, "What to Do with Reclaimed Instructional Time" in *Testing Too Much? A Principal's Guide to Cutting Back Testing and Reclaiming Instructional Time* by Philip A. Streifer with Barry G. Sheckley and Richard Ayers (Lanham, MD: Rowan and Littlefield, 2017), 125–142.

the most research-based and experiential elementary experience possible. Barry's research shows that when we experience the concepts we are learning, our brains retain the knowledge and we gain deeper understanding. He has taught UP Academy's leaders and educators how to shape our school's environment, how to talk with students and trust them with agency over their education, and when to provide structure. Much of what I share in *Rebel Educator* I have learned from him, and some of his stories appear in these pages.

I have also been fortunate to be surrounded by exceptional educators who create classrooms of agency and have shared their knowledge with me and UP Academy to make these ideas and our school a success.

It's not what we can teach our students to be when they grow up—it's how we support them in learning to solve the problems that matter most in their worlds, and ours.

Create a classroom where impact and imagination meet. Be a Rebel Educator.

WHAT WOULD MAKE YOUR JOB BETTER?

"

The ability to teach my subject in a way that builds confidence in my students and allows them to actually learn, think, and create. Not just pander to some test. Oh, and being treated and paid like a professional.

"

—Melissa, fourteen-year veteran teacher

CHAPTER 1

THE TEACHING QUANDARY

PACT—LEARNING EDUCATION BY VOLUNTEERING

My girls attended a parent participation, project-based public school. Parents volunteered in the classroom assisting or teaching two hours per week. In addition, we served on a committee and volunteered for the school's annual events. I was excited to be a part of my children's education, but the real reason I chose this school was for my oldest daughter. Eliza was born with cerebral palsy and couldn't walk or talk. She needed full support to participate in class, which meant she needed a full-time aide that was not me. I thought her having a one-on-one aide would seem less different in a class where many adults actively participated in the classroom; everyone's parent or caregiver volunteered in the class for a few hours each week. I felt it would help her fit in and also give me the opportunity to observe how school was going for her. I had no idea about the other benefits, both to me and to Eliza. I had no idea that volunteering in this classroom would lead me into a career in education and launching my own school.

The school required all parents to take training. This was one of the committee jobs, and other parents and educators who had worked with the school longer provided the training. We learned the basics of Responsive Classroom and classroom management and the teachers' different schedules and styles.

One activity that stands out in my mind is the idea of a "good boy." When talking about kids, parents and teachers often refer to students as good boys or good girls (or other labels). So what is a "good boy"? In this exercise, we were challenged to answer this question. Is it someone who sits quietly in class? Someone who answers questions when asked? Someone who cleans up his messes? A good boy may be all of these things and more, but what is important to remember is that all students are good boys (and girls). They may be learning to deal with feelings, or to control reactions; they may be coming to school while facing abuse, trauma, disabilities, and a host of other challenges we don't see in their eyes and on their faces, but they are all good kids. It's how we manage the classroom—the lessons, the culture, and the relationship that we build—that make the difference.

After the training, learning, and interacting with other parents, I felt a little terrified to walk into a room of twenty-seven five-year-olds. My business coach would call the feeling "scarecited"—I was scared and excited. I had been asked to teach PE. I have a background in teaching dance, mountain biking, and snowboarding plus a yoga teaching certification, and Eliza's teacher had decided I was qualified. But I had never taught kids, and definitely not twenty-seven of them at once. On the first day, I decided to teach soccer, which was ironic because I had no background in that sport. However, a bag of size 3 balls had been donated to the school and my daughter was taking a kids soccer class. I paid attention each week and copied what her weekend coach did with the three-year-olds and did the same thing with my five-year-olds. It worked brilliantly, until the day we needed to form a circle, holding hands. The kids started pulling, pushing, running forward and back, breaking the circle and not focusing. Holding hands and making a circle had too many directions. It took us the full thirty minutes, and we didn't get to move on to any other activities. We never made a complete circle, but we did have lots of frustration and lots of laughs.

What I learned that year wasn't from teaching PE; it was from subbing for other parents in the classroom. If a parent couldn't make a shift, it was our responsibility to find someone to fill in for us. On one such occasion, I taught a lesson from the Kid Writing curriculum.[2] English Language Arts was taught in activity centers with each group of students grouped by their level of understanding and mastery of the subject. As any educator knows, in any class of students, whether a mixed-age class or one with students the same age, there is a wide range of understanding and mastery. Some kindergarteners come to school already reading; for some it will take until second or third grade for them to read comfortably; others have reading challenges that will need extra attention.

---

2   More information about the Kid Writing curriculum, which was developed by Eileen Feldgus, Isabell Cardonick, and J. Richard Gentry, can be found at *www.kidwriting.com*.

That day, I was at the rainbow table with the kids, their journals, and a writing prompt. Each day they used a different writing implement designed to strengthen their fine motor skills and a writing prompt designed to give them inspiration. The idea behind "kid writing" is to reinforce what students know and stretch them to develop their writing skills. Students start by drawing a picture; then they write a story about it. As kindergarteners, they don't yet have the writing, phonemic, and letter knowledge to write a full story, so they write any letters they hear in the words of their story. Then they make "magic lines" for any letters or sounds they don't know. This encourages them to sound out words, recognize sounds, and write any letters they hear. As an adult who was not an educator, I thought it was a fascinating way to learn to write. It gives the students a way to see their progress from the beginning of the year to the end.

Sitting at that table and "adult writing" twenty-seven kids' stories was amazing. Let me explain "adult writing": the students kid write, then they share their story with an adult, who writes their words under their "magic lines." The adult underlines any letters the students correctly identified. In this way, students see their work, remember their story, and gain validation of their knowledge. The assignment isn't to identify what is right or wrong about their writing; it is meant to bring attention to the process and highlight the letters and words the student got correct.

I remember reading and hearing the students' ideas and being in awe of their creativity and learning. I left that day with a smile on my face. Talking about it later with my husband, I recounted that I now understood why people become teachers. Through this experience, I saw how kids are amazingly fun, full of energy, and creative. I had come from never wanting to have children to wanting to be around them every day.

WHY BE A TEACHER

Most teachers I have met decided on their careers because they wanted to change the world. They wanted to make a difference; they wanted to help. They understood that the way to do this was to support and mentor youth. All the teachers I have met, and maybe those you know too, want to make the world a better place. They aim to improve the lives of students, to make a connection with "that one kid," and to influence and support all the others. It's a profession where the days are long, but the years are short. Conversely, the class periods are often too short and the work expected of them bleeds into every aspect of their lives. Teachers grade papers on breaks, read essays around the campfire, and spend summers doing professional development. Good teachers who build relationships with their students and care deeply about their outcomes never really take a break. They are always thinking about their students and how to help them become the best they can be.

Every day brings the possibility of new wonder, questions, innovations, creativity, and the chance to make a difference. Students make new connections between information and their lives each day, and teachers get to watch those light bulbs go off. Teachers literally get to see their students' brains making new connections. Lives change because of their influence. What an incredible profession!

But it's not all glamorous. Working with kids is challenging. They lose teeth, get hurt and bleed, they throw up on the floor. They experience big emotions they don't understand. They haven't learned how to work through their feelings, or they have been taught faulty coping mechanisms that are difficult to reframe. Humans are messy creatures in general, and building little humans is messy and challenging work. Understanding the humanity of the profession, curriculum choices can be just as challenging.

For educators who teach the same grade or class in the same school year after year, the curriculum can get monotonous. They help different little humans each year learn to understand the world around them, which makes the monotony worth it. But the curriculum and what educators are expected to teach don't change often. This is both a gift and a curse. The cyclical nature of teaching means an educator who instructs the same grade level teaches the same lessons and the same curriculum each year. The students change, but the curriculum doesn't.

Many teachers continually ask, "How can we best serve each new group of students with the same curriculum? The world is rapidly changing, shouldn't our education methods be changing as well?" If this has been a source of frustration for you, this book can help. We will explore ways to shift the curriculum and focus, while still keeping true to teaching the concepts students need to learn. As an educational system, should we be teaching the same things over and over to humans who are all so different? Or should we find new ways to teach concepts, ways that match the personalities and interests of each group of students? My fellow Rebel Educator, you already know the answer.

As humans, we crave challenges. We need to see things in new ways and learn (and teach) from new perspectives. We don't need to teach the same things in the same way year after year. We can teach the same curriculum in new ways. We can adapt the skills students need to the interests of each class. We can teach different content but the same concepts. When we use an inquiry- and concept-based system, every year brings a new challenge to connect and create with a new group of students.

Many teachers spend time in university and masters programs designing innovative curriculum and learning about the ways students learn best. They may be dismayed to discover many districts and administrators ask that they teach a standard curriculum—not one based on the most recent science of learning but often the same one that has been taught for years.

Standardized testing, which the government put into practice to serve as a yardstick for progress and funding, creates another hurdle. Educators are asked to "teach to the test" instead of expanding the experiences and the thinking of their students. Teachers feel pressure for students to attain a certain grade level for the school to remain competitive or continue to receive a level of funding. These teachers (maybe this is you) feel drained each day, like they are trying to fill an empty jar with pebbles that are just a little too big to fit. The pebbles won't go in, but the teacher is expected to keep pushing, until one day the jar shatters and the teacher leaves the profession.

Educators are told to impart knowledge that students need to know for a reason that is important to the school—the test—but not important to the student. If learning isn't important to the student, they become resistant. They fall asleep in class, act out, don't show up, are not engaged, and don't care. This is the opposite of what school should look like. And in response, many teachers suffer from burnout and depression. Many change careers.

I surveyed almost one hundred teachers from around the country when writing this book. Only fourteen of them said they had never considered leaving the profession. This means 80 percent of teachers at any given school are thinking of quitting. Ironically, teachers mentioned bureaucracy both as the reason they want to leave and the reason they stay. Many feel micromanaged. They hate "teaching to the test" and seeing the limited resources schools have used to force mandatory testing. Many stayed for the benefits, the pensions, and the summers "off."

In the survey, I asked teachers what they love about teaching. Here are a few of their responses:

"That 'ah ha' moment when a student has been working so hard and finally gets it," says Andrea, a teacher of seventeen years.

"Loving the children, knowing that for some of them, I am the only adult who ever shows/tells them that I love them and they are worth my time," shares Jennifer Godfrey.

They are also aware of the challenges. Arlene Cleary says, "Job security is easily the most difficult challenge I have faced. Teachers have so many responsibilities now. We differentiate, create, purchase, or tweak materials to make them more challenging, interesting, hands on, multisensory, include several learning styles, incorporate technology in a meaningful way. We incorporate behavior management strategies into our everyday life and are held responsible for behavior outside of the classroom. We are nurses to students with scrapes and cuts and belly aches. We are the parents of anywhere from twenty-two to thirty students (lower elementary). We contact parents for negative and positive behavior. We spend our nights awake and worried about our kids. We dedicate our spare time to after-school clubs and activities. We spend any free time we get planning lessons, and it's still not enough to keep your job."

With so much pressure on teachers, it's hard to focus on what matters: relationships and learning. A theme I heard over and over in my survey was the lack of respect and time and the overwhelming amount of challenges.

Our educators are raising a generation of young leaders. With the rise of dual-income families and the migration away from extended families, teachers are often the adults students see most during the day. In addition to academics, they teach social and emotional skills, character traits, and instill a sense of self and security in our youth. They are professionals who deserve autonomy, trust, and respect. They also deserve the latitude to use their knowledge and creativity in the classroom to make our students the best they can be. Until we allow these things for teachers, can we really expect teachers to create them for our children?

THE EVOLUTION OF SCHOOL

To quote the late Sir Ken Robinson, *New York Times* bestselling author who led national and international projects on creative and cultural education across the world,

"Imagination is the source of every form of human achievement. And it's the one thing that I believe we are systematically jeopardizing in the way we educate our children and ourselves."

But how did we get to this point? Let's take a look at how our education system evolved.

In the 1600s, most students learned at home with their families. By the mid part of that century, it was decided that all towns of one hundred or more people should have a Latin school, to promote reading of the Bible. By the late 1700s, we began to see the groundwork being laid for our current system of schooling. Jefferson proposed that there be two tracks to schooling: one for the laboring and one for the learned. Does this sound familiar? Does your school separate children into some sort of track? This idea is almost four hundred years old, and we are still segregating students.

In the early 1800s, we started to see public schools opening that were free for all students. But parents were skeptical, and it took several decades to catch on. In the mid-1800s, the first kindergartens opened and the Department of Education was formed. Fifty years later, property taxes started paying for schools, a practice that has set up some schools for success and others for failure, depending on the property values surrounding the schools. While all states still rely on property taxes to fund schools, each state varies how they use this funding today.

Most public schools have a learning pipeline in place. Students are placed into tracks based on current performance and knowledge; this allows some to excel but leaves others to wither. Looking back in history, this idea of putting students in a "track" was originally designed to keep some students from excelling. The white, wealthy land and business owners wanted educated workers, but not so educated that they would have their own ideas. Education began tracking students to be sure that some (white, wealthy) students had the education to go to college or run businesses and some (everyone else) had just enough education to function in society, follow orders, and become workers. Our schools were not designed to help everyone to reach their potential or succeed. As a society, we created further disparity by funding schools through property taxes. Wealthy areas have more tax revenue, more money for schools, and more resources to fund better schools. Poor areas have the opposite.

We could deep dive into the equity issues of school funding through property taxes, school size, and track learning, but that is for another book. What is of note is that our funding structure for schools has not fundamentally changed in almost 250 years. However, our objectives as a society and the demands of an ever-changing world have changed dramatically.

It wasn't until the early 1900s that we saw education offered to students of all races and heritage. It's important to note that this education was not equal among everyone; in fact, it was still designed to be unequal. In the early 1900s, the goal of education was to teach as many as possible, as efficiently as possible so people could become good factory workers for the industrial rise in the United States. It could be argued that education was actually used to keep people from moving up the social ladder. People were only taught the necessary skills for blue-collar jobs. Schools did not teach the creativity, free thinking, and problem-solving skills needed to advance in the workplace.

More recently, as the United States struggles to reclaim its place in the top ten countries in the world for education (in 1990, it was sixth; in 2018, it was 27th, according to the Institute for Health Metrics and Evaluation), our presidents have begun numerous educational efforts. These include Bill Clinton's Improving America's

Schools Act, George W. Bush's No Child Left Behind, and Barack Obama's Race to the Top initiatives. In its desperate push, the US has worked to create a national curriculum. This has taken autonomy away from the states and educators and pushed a national agenda designed to create a framework of what students need to learn in school. The Common Core was created in 2009 to do this work, and standardized testing was increased to track its progress. The educational system focused on ensuring students in all schools received the same curriculum. Schools became more standardized so all students would have the same advantages of an American education. Based on the US's fall in global educational standing, it is clear these efforts largely haven't worked.

There are several reasons for this: The national agenda of common standards and standardized testing undermines the freedom and creativity of our nation's amazing teachers. The system of supporting schools with property taxes creates more inequity in the system as higher property value areas receive more property tax money, while poorer areas receive less. The federal government has not filled in the gap and funded education or worked to equivalize school funding.

Any educator can tell you they teach for the students, not the paycheck. In countries that truly value education, teachers are paid professional wages. The US has cut education budgets annually by as much as 3 percent since 2008, while student populations grow and states demand more and better test scores. This leads to larger class sizes, more educator stress, and more student burnout. None of these things leads to a fulfilling workplace for the educator or successful and innovative environments for the students.

Neuroscience of Learning

As we move beyond history and into the future, what mistakes should we avoid? What can we leave behind and what can we learn from?

It is well-accepted science that we learn the best when we can hear, do, experience, and teach. The highest form of mastery is being able to teach others. The neuroscience of learning allows us to understand that we have deeper learning when we experience the concepts we learn about, and we master them when we teach others. We know we question and learn more deeply when our brains and body are in a state of disruption. This state occurs when something has changed in our environment, our thinking, or our body that makes us stop and say, "Wait, what?!" In those moments, we become engaged. We do this naturally. It happens when we manipulate objects or images, when we learn with our physical bodies and our minds, or when we are experiencing and thinking.

I invite you to take a moment and think back to elementary school. Think of a memory of learning there. Go ahead, close your eyes and think of something that stands out. It might be a lesson, a teacher, or a field trip. Most likely, you thought of a time where you were taught in a different way. Maybe your teacher did something unconventional in the classroom. It might have been a field trip or an in-class project. We remember best the discrepancies, the things that altered our state of learning.

I'll share one of my memories. When I was in second grade, the class across the hall had an aquarium where tadpoles were growing into frogs. I went into the class every spare moment I was allowed. I wanted to see the frogs growing up. It wasn't even my lesson, but aside from never passing my timed division tests in third grade, this is one of the most vivid memories I have—because it was different; it challenged the physical and mental and put them in a state of disruption. I learned and retained more deeply than I would have by reading about tadpoles and looking at pictures of growing frogs in a book.

This is our goal as educators every day: to create lessons that have meaning, impact lives, and are memorable so our students can use that knowledge as they grow. You don't have to grow frogs to do this, but I found it memorable.

We live in a world where information and content are everywhere. We must use the neuroscience of learning to advance and support our students. We need to use the tricks we know lead to deeper understanding. We can literally ask Siri anything. We can quickly google information we don't know. Content is everywhere. How students decipher it, what they can do with it, and how they think critically, creatively, and collaboratively will lead to their future success. We don't need to teach content; rather, we need to offer experiences to build relationships and skills that build on knowledge. We have to give today's students an education that will help them succeed in the future, not in the past.

Allow me to share another memory of school to illustrate this idea. I remember an art class (and I hated art) where we took a field trip and walked downtown to draw perspective. We were each asked to sit in a different spot and draw the same building. We were given time to fill in the details, we were outside in a new environment, and we were encouraged to draw exactly what we saw. I was proud of that drawing; it was the best drawing I had ever done. Our teacher had created a discrepancy. We weren't in the same art studio; we were in a different environment.

I also remember a project in my tenth-grade history class: we had a choice to take a test or write creative historical fiction. I wrote a love story set during the Revolutionary War (I was, and still am, a romantic). My teacher liked it so much that he asked me if I would be comfortable reading it to the class. I did. There wasn't a dry eye in the classroom. He told me I was the only one that year who did the writing option. I don't remember the details or dates of the Revolutionary War (despite recently watching *Hamilton*), and I doubt my classmates do either, even though they were tested on them. I remember the way I felt, the freedom of creativity and the ability to be trusted to do something different. That is what we should be creating for our students—trust in their own creativity.

Let's go back to the things you remember most from school. Do you remember that amazing lecture from tenth grade history? (I remember sleeping a lot in that class.) Do you remember sitting at the table in first grade learning phonics and sight words? If you're like me, you don't recall those things, but that doesn't mean they weren't important. I can read, and I can write this book because my first grade teacher taught me letter sounds and how they combine to make words. Even though those aren't the memories that stick with me, they allow me to learn more things. Both of these types of learning are important: the things we need to know to build upon and the things that create experiences we remember. As educators, how we combine the "need to know" with the "fun to know" or "want to know" makes all the difference.

These educators, in these moments I shared, allowed for deeper learning. They allowed a love of the subject matter to shine through; they allowed for the spark of learning. What if we, as educators, did that all the time, as a philosophy of teaching, not just once a year as a blip in the curriculum? What if that *was* the curriculum? What would students remember then?

Creating experiences in learning is more engaging and enriching for both educators and students. We can avoid much of the educator burnout by creating supportive schools and systems that invite creativity. We can support our educators by inviting innovative professional development. We can give our professional teachers the time and trust to create for our students.

How is your school doing? Are there changes that could be made? Do the changes come from the superintendent, the principal, the PTA, or could they come from each individual teacher?

There are different ways to start a revolution. You can attack from the top, try to topple the system and overtake it, which is messy and violent. Or you can create a thousand points of difference and dissonance. Many small parts add pressure to change the whole. Every teacher can make a difference. Every teacher can change the world. It is possible within the confines and constraints of our current system. But we need to be creative; we need to do things in new ways. We need a revolution in education. We need to be Rebel Educators.

TEACHING FROM THE HEART

We must pay respect to the emotional aspect of teaching. Teaching is not just any career, as any teacher can tell you. This cannot be overlooked or overstated. Educators become a part of each of their student's families. They build a new classroom into a family every year. They serve as a key caregiver for younger students and a trusted confidant for older ones. They not only relay information, but they also teach students how to become good people. They are mediators, negotiators, and therapists. They step into situations that are dangerous to students either indirectly, by calling other authorities, or sometimes directly, putting themselves in danger.

This is a career where each year there are more students to get to know, to develop into little (or big) humans, and to love. This takes a huge emotional toll. Teaching isn't an office marketing job. In marketing, if no one likes your ad campaign, you might get fired, but (most likely) no one truly gets hurt. When teachers respond insensitively or miss signs of abuse, it can cause scars that last a lifetime.

Our teachers are raising a generation. It is a big responsibility, and for the educators who take their job seriously and understand the gravity of their actions, it can be a big weight. The best teachers recognize that their words and actions may influence what a student chooses, or doesn't choose, to do in life. Often their words influence how a student feels about different skills, knowledge, careers, and themselves. Without offering appropriate professional and personal development for educators, even the best schools will see educators burn out from emotional exhaustion, career fatigue, and overwork. This shatters the dream of what each teacher thought their work would be.

I asked teachers, "What is the hardest part about being a teacher?"

"All the stuff that doesn't have to do with interacting with the kids. Report cards, ridiculous lesson plans, meetings. The hardest is when the school system puts demands on you and your students that you know are not in the best interest of your kids. There are a lot of very specific directions on how to do things, which is a shame because I think kids get a lot more when each teacher can truly teach their own way," shares Kristina Rilee.

Despite the drawbacks, it's still the best career on the planet. The opportunity to make a difference and change the world presents itself almost daily. Teachers are some of the most innovative and creative people on Earth. Let's give them the opportunity to highlight those traits and use their skills to develop our children into the best they can be—so both teachers and students can reach their ultimate potential.

"In the classroom, when I watch students working together on something difficult and they are immersed in the moment of learning and discovery, I disappear into the background and they work together to gain understanding."

—Aimée Skidmore

WHY DID YOU BECOME A TEACHER?

> "
> I believe that education is the start of any solution to any problem. I wanted to be a part of solving problems.
> "

—Anonymous veteran educator
of twenty-one years

CHAPTER 2

A CENTURY OF PASSIVE LEARNERS

BUILDING ACTIVE LEARNERS

Our current method of teaching and our system of seat time—counting the hours and days spent in a classroom—are relics of a bygone era. But we still use them. Schools are still judged by them. We all know that the amount of time you sit in a seat does not determine the amount of information or skills you learn. In fact, it could be argued that the more time spent sitting, the less we actually learn. Students in classes where they have little agency have more difficulty making decisions for themselves. Even in progressive schools, students can be seen raising their hand to throw away a piece of garbage or get a fresh piece of paper. This type of educator control is not conducive to raising students who have their own agency. It does not teach students to take responsibility for their own learning, or problem solve effectively, because even small decisions are being made for them. We need to find ways to balance autonomy with structure to create the classrooms of the future.

The majority of education in this country is designed around our history of farming and factories. School starts at eight or nine, after morning chores, and is done around three so students can work in the fields after the hot noontime sun. We have summers off for the growing season and harvest. Don't get me wrong, I love having summers off. But if we look at the majority of today's parents, they work year-round; they work office hours, roughly nine to five. If our schools are intended to support the American family schedule, that is not how they are currently functioning.

The way we educate once we are in the classroom was designed to produce factory workers. The "tracks" we created were designed to separate students of means, who could go to college, from students who were destined to become workers in the "system." This system was designed to create employees who wouldn't question why or what was being done, to create employees who would follow directions, show up on time, and not complain or cause trouble. But most of our factories are gone. Those that remain are looking for efficiencies, for employees who can engineer a solution to a problem, for people who can program a robot to do the job correctly.

The jobs of 2020 are very different from those of 1920, and we can assume that the jobs in 2080 will be even more so. To meet the demands of those future jobs, our educational system needs to change. Our generation of passive learners needs to take charge and become solution-minded problem solvers. We need to build active learners, and get students involved and caring about their education. And as educators, we need to teach the things they care about.

The way to do this is to design active learning spaces and experiences. One of the best examples of this is Ramona Pierson. Ramona is an education pioneer who created SynapticMash, an education software company that she sold to Promethean, and Declara, an internet company created to connect educators and educational institutions to information and collaboration. She also spent a brief time on the board of directors at UP Academy. In 1984, when she was in her twenties, Ramona went for a run with her dog. As she crossed a road in a crosswalk, she was hit head-on by a driver who ran a red light. Her body was mangled as her leg caught up in the front axle of the automobile. Her dog was killed instantly. Ramona survived but was in a coma for the next eighteen months. When she awoke, she was blind. She learned to read Braille, to use a cane, and had a see-ing-eye dog. Eleven years later, she learned of an experi-mental new surgery that could restore her sight. She was initially reluctant (she liked exploring the world with a dog), but ultimately decided to give it a try. Experimental surgeries had rebuilt her body after the accident, and she had faith in them. She underwent brain and eye surgery with the hope of seeing again, and it was a suc-cess. The world Ramona saw was quite different from the one she'd experienced eleven years prior. Computers were everywhere; even cell phones had become hand-held computers. Architecture had changed, fashion and trends had evolved. But when she walked into a school, it was exactly the same. She had the vision to see all the changes in the world, and the stagnation of education. It led her to found two education companies, and is an example of why education should evolve with society.

CHANGING EDUCATION FOR THE FUTURE OF WORK

In sales, we are told the most dangerous words are "because that's the way we've always done it." If a company has this mentality, it will soon be left behind, forgotten, and out of business. But that is exactly the mentality we have in education. Many of us think, *It worked well enough for me, so it is fine for my children*, while in the next breath we acknowledge that most of what we learned in school wasn't particularly useful. We don't remember all those facts that were so important to memorize for the test. And we know the world has changed; it is not the same as it was when we were kids. There is new technology, new ways to communicate, new ways to design, and new ways to make a living.

It was good enough for me, but is good enough really enough? Don't our children, our students, deserve better than good enough? What if we created lessons that consistently combine concepts with experiences? What if we made all learning relevant and took subjects out of silos? What if we gave students an understanding of why the subjects they were learning are important and how they work together? Instead of giving them a "good enough" education, what if we gave them the best we had to offer? The next generation would be unstoppable.

When we look at the future of work, we see the divergence and decoupling of industries and professions that were once combined. We see marketing companies separate from the corporations that build the product; editing companies separate from publishing houses; independent drivers for deliveries, human rides, and packages. The "gig economy" is growing, and it uses skills that are not "sit, listen, follow directions." The skills this new economy uses are entrepreneurial. They derive from scientific minds. They are collaborative and creative. Those who find success in this new era of work have developed skill sets to market themselves, and they have learned to create opportunities and be flexible. They become chameleons, changing into what is needed at the moment, retooling their skills when societal or market needs change. They are always learning.

As stated in "Schools of the Future: Defining New Models of Education for the Fourth Industrial Revolution," the January 2020 report from the World Economic Forum, "There is an urgent need to update education systems to equip children with the skills to navigate the future of work and the future of societies." Students need a "cocktail" of skills—technology mixed with cooking, math mixed with gardening. They will need to understand the "soft skills" and learn how to learn, stay curious, and keep learning. When we teach this way—not in silos, but combining subjects into life experiences—we give our students an advantage in the game of life.

As educators, we are still largely working within the confines of a district or a system that hasn't changed. How do we, then, make changes in our classrooms that will have a positive influence on the next generation? One answer may come from the current pandemic. As I write this, we are under a shelter in place order and are unable to attend regular school. Schools find themselves forced to change how they do things, to look at what is important to learn and shift priorities. When we have limited student attention on video conferencing and shortened time with them during the day, it means we have to shift our priorities. For many schools and educators, this became support and connection with other humans; academics came second. We already knew that relationships are incredibly important to growing children. We learned that when you build those relationships and trust in your students, there are many different forms education can take.

I hear a lot of discussion around reimagining what school could look like. I am hopeful, as I imagine you are, too, that some of these changes will stay—that schools could be judged on their students mastering competencies instead of memorizing facts. That students will be able to take the lead in what they are learning and study areas of interest. Time will tell how this shift will change education in the future.

BECOMING A LEARNING FACILITATOR

For teachers, becoming a learning facilitator instead of a "sage on the stage" can be a scary place. It means surrendering control of the daily curriculum. It releases the structure of students always being at their desk, in their place, and raising their hands. It shifts how we view the dissemination of information. Many educators see themselves as the experts, filling heads with information that students revisit on a test. When we shift learning to become student-centered, the educator is more like a coach. They facilitate learning, ask driving questions, and steer the research efforts. They develop a learner. For many teachers, this is the dream—the learning that drives the spark they love to see. This is what engages and ignites students and gets them excited. When teachers make this shift from educator to coach, from giver of information to facilitator and engineer of learning, our students move from being factory copies to independent thinkers.

Let's look at a classroom example that Barry Sheckley, Ph.D., shares with us about a kindergarten teacher who wanted her students to be more independent.[3] This educator's methods made an unforgettable impact. I call this the clothespin story. The teacher wanted her students to stop constantly asking her what they were supposed to be doing. Maybe as an educator you've had this experience: you explain the assignment, the students appropriately respond with what to do next, then your class moves to do it and half the students come and ask you what to do. This teacher wanted structure in her class, but also to give her students autonomy. She wanted to find a way to celebrate common class goals, but also to recognize personal accomplishments. So she developed a system of clotheslines and clothespins that is genius.

Imagine that you are walking into her classroom. You see tables in the center arranged as workstations and individual student desks scattered around a larger area. Along the perimeter, on the walls at about three feet high, kindergarten height, there are clotheslines looped and hanging. Each line has a clothespin, a set of activities, worksheets, and plans for the day. There is one for

---

3   This story is taken from Sheckley, "What to Do with Reclaimed Instructional Time."

each student, each line labeled with a student's name. When the students come in, they go to their clothesline and choose an activity. They might work with a partner or find a manipulative to work with. Maybe they play a game in an activity center or they go back to their desk to quietly work on their sight words. The room is abuzz with movement and learning—students working together and alone, students conferencing with their teacher. When they have finished an activity or mastered a lesson, the students check in with their teacher to confirm the activity is correct and complete. The teacher gives them feedback, information, lessons, or confirmation. The student can put a star next to each item they complete on the daily task board, which has each task and each student's name listed on a large chart. When the whole class completes a row of tasks, they walk together to the master task board in the hallway and celebrate completing the class task goal by putting a star on the master board.

Each day, students have new activities and tasks on their clothesline, but they know what to expect. They will be challenged, have ownership of their learning, and have the freedom to decide what to learn and in what order. Most importantly, their teacher is there to guide and facilitate their learning. She answers questions and corrects mistakes so students become confident in their ability to make decisions and trust that they can learn material independently. She creates autonomy and structure that enables both her and her students to enjoy the learning experience. And, remember dear reader, this is a kindergarten class. Imagine what is possible as these students grow.

The design of this teacher's classroom clearly illustrates her trust in her students and her ability to give them responsibility for their learning. Trust and responsibility are two major character traits sorely missing in many of our general classrooms where a teacher talks and students are expected to sit quietly and listen. We need to give our students responsibility for their learning and trust that they are capable learners. Two major elements make this example a success: the responsibility and social maturity of her students, and the environment she has created.

USING SOCIAL-EMOTIONAL DEVELOPMENT, ENVIRONMENT, AND COMPETENCY TO CREATE ACTIVE LEARNERS

Daniel Goleman, Ph.D., author of the *New York Times* bestseller *Emotional Intelligence* and *Social Intelligence: The New Science of Human Relationships*, is a leader in the social-emotional development education space. When we look at his work, we see a focus on noticing emotion, validating that emotion, then choosing the response to the emotion. In a school setting, this is done in many ways. Some schools use social-emotional curriculums, such as Zones of Regulation or the YMCA Cornerstone program. These are often taught for an hour once a month by someone who comes into the classroom to share information and perhaps offers an activity before leaving. The teachers engaged in this process use that visit through the coming weeks to illustrate struggles, conflict resolution, kindness, and other lessons.

Some teachers may not have the time, knowledge, or bandwidth to fully incorporate the lessons into the classroom without more professional development and incentive to make it happen. But that doesn't mean that social-emotional development and growth isn't happening. It occurs every day when educators talk with students about their feelings about an incident, an assignment, or something another student said; when they mediate arguments or discussions between students; when they offer advice and support. And these moments are some of what educators went into teaching for—to help students grow, personally and academically. Educators who are empowered with tools to help their students develop holistically are more engaged, happier, and fulfilled. These tools create moments for social- emotional growth within the daily happenings of the school. They build environments for student agency and assume competency from all students and trust in their abilities.

Many schools, including UP Academy, use this approach. When we began, we had an SEL (social-emotional learning) educator come once a week and do a lesson. Parents liked the idea and students enjoyed it. But this was just checking the SEL box. We found that it didn't trickle into the classroom culture as readily as we would have liked, and students didn't have a full understanding of the stories and lessons. They didn't transfer the story to their lives without ongoing reminding and instruction. In order to make this part of the fabric of the school and part of the driving culture, it became necessary to make the switch to having SEL training for educators so they could provide the lessons themselves. This includes content, lesson plans, and ideas for incorporating the language and culture into the classroom. When educators provided the lessons and thoroughly understood the importance of its repetition, it became part of the school vocabulary and culture. In this way, students understand that they are always learning, growing and connected to those around them. It also gives educators the tools to better support their students' social-emotional development.

The importance of setting up the classroom environment, creating community, and building relationships cannot be overstated. Educators must set up their classrooms to provide a welcoming, supportive, non-threatening, inclusive, equitable, non-biased setting for students' learning. This includes making time daily for students to express their feelings, thoughts, ideas, triumphs, and struggles. It includes creating classroom agreements and values that we consistently live by. We must create psychologically safe spaces in our classrooms for our students. When we model that behavior and create the environment, our students are free to develop their social-emotional skills in a safe space. Classrooms must be set up to support students' social-emotional needs and, in turn, educators must provide instruction that develops students' skills in establishing and sustaining their own social-emotional well-being.

Providing the vocabulary for students to have agency and ask for help is important. Giving students a solid base of social-emotional ability to share their feelings and thoughts is part of that process. If a student is unable to express their frustration, how can they express that they need help? If a student cannot understand and process the difference between confusion and dislike, how can they advocate for taking a different approach to the subject? Students need to learn the language, see how it's used through modeling, and feel safe in their environment to share their emotions—whether these emotions are frustration, anger, confusion, misunderstanding, or the happiness and excitement that comes with the ease of an assignment and joy of learning. Social-emotional education and maturity gives us this ability so when a student is in a classroom environment built for agency, they have the tools to explore and learn.

Along with building a healthy social-emotional culture in the classroom, we also need an environment built to create active learners. I gave the example of Dr. Sheckley's clothespin story, but there are many other examples of this. In the classroom, they range from having a choice table to allowing students to choose their own schedule.

Early on at UP Academy, we created afternoon Flexible Learning Time. We decided as a classroom group what the students wanted to focus on—in this case, an animal in a biome and building something with wood. Our afternoons were also our time for math. As the educator,

I laid out the steps in each project and the math chapters we needed to cover over the semester. Each week, I shared with the students what we needed to work on and what we needed to complete that week. We decided together each day what to work on. We are all human, and we don't always want to do the same thing each day. When given a choice, some days the students felt like writing and some days they felt like building. They were more engaged and involved in their learning. The subject matter was in line with their rhythms, and they had a choice about what they were learning. They had chosen the projects and also chose when to work on them.

Creating a learning environment where students can choose what to work on and when to work on it is a powerful tool for educators to harness. It builds agency and engagement in the students while building relationships and trust within the class.

The last piece of moving from passive learning to active participants in learning is assuming competency from our students. Students need to have the emotional maturity to make decisions about their learning, an environment conducive to supporting their decisions, and knowing they are trusted to make those decisions. Often we have ideas about what students can accomplish or what they are capable of. This situation is most glaringly obvious in special education students, but it happens with all students. The teacher is the expert, which means the students are "less than," or not capable and not competent. We all have implicit biases that make this difficult. Sometimes it is a diagnosis, a reputation, a sibling, or the color of the student's skin, but we can't let our bias get in the way of our students' success. Teachers often speak to students in a way that insinuates they need to listen and follow rules instead of question and be curious. When we move from demanding respect to giving mutual respect, students respond. It is important that we respect our students and speak to them as little humans. When they are given higher expectations, and when we believe they are competent to reach them, then our students really shine.

THE EXPECTATION GAP

In the United States, our special needs students are often put into separate classrooms. They are not given the opportunity to share what they know or learn a general education curriculum alongside their peers. Sometimes it's because of communication struggles, behavior struggles, or a school policy or procedure. The subtle, or sometimes not so subtle, message these students are told from the beginning of their educational careers is that they are not smart, strong, or good enough to learn the same as their peers. That is a strong negative message to give to any student.

Whether students are placed in separate classrooms or inclusive environments, they often have different expectations. Sometimes this is because of their race, who their older sibling was, an incident from a previous class, or a diagnosis. Even the best, most equitable educators have biases. It becomes apparent when a teacher looks at their class list and notices a last name—*I hope he's quieter than his brother*, they think. Or they see an IEP (Individual Education Plan) that accompanies a student and shares behavior and accommodation expectations. As humans, we relate these things with experiences we have had or what we have been taught to expect. Our thoughts and expectations might be lower than what a student is actually capable of. All humans are different, all humans with the same diagnosis are different, and all humans with the same last name are different. When we change our expectations, whether consciously or unconsciously, based on something we think we know about someone, we immediately create a gap between what we think this student can accomplish and what they might actually be able to accomplish. This is the expectation gap. It stops capable students from reaching their potential.

When we look at our students with disabilities, the expectation gap becomes even greater. I'll use my daughter Eliza as an example. She read above grade level and did three-digit math in first grade. She had cerebral palsy and couldn't walk or talk. The expectation was that she wouldn't graduate. Even though she was a student proving her academic ability, our educational system wanted to take away her ability to graduate with a diploma—take away her future at six years old. In the United States, students with disabilities have the option to go to school until they are twenty-two and finish with a certificate of completion. This is not a diploma and will not get a student into college. What happens when we shift from our expectations of students to look at their strengths and possibilities? In my daughter's case, it would mean looking at her high aptitude for academics and how well she tried to communicate instead of looking at what she couldn't do—walk and talk.

We continue to see students thrive after being taken out of the special day class and given a chance in an inclusive classroom. These students are catching up with peers in learning and going to college. They blame special education for keeping them from reaching their potential earlier. In the words of Rachel Kripke-Ludwig, a student with autism, "It was the unconscious biases of special educators that held me back. They were taught that I cannot learn, so they did not provide grade-level lessons. But I can and must learn everything other kids do. Knowledge is power. Keeping me from information disempowers me and causes anxiety. It guarantees my second-class status."[4] Inclusion may not work for every student, but I argue that in the vast majority of cases, if we can create the proper class size for student attention and the school allows for the correct support, most students will thrive with their peers.

My daughter was fortunate to be in a general education classroom. We advocated to give her the opportunity to learn, even though she couldn't walk or talk. By being with her peers, she was in the top half of her class in reading, in the high math group, accomplishing things some of her able-bodied peers struggled with. She was social, observant, intelligent, and curious. I am confident that if she had been put in a secluded special day class, she would have been one of the kids banging their head against a tray and biting their arms because they were bored, not because they had behavior problems. But if that had happened, and she did develop those behaviors,

4   Rachel Kripke-Ludwig, "Believe in Me: Insights of a Nonspeaking College-Bound Autistic," *Autism in Adulthood* 2 no. 2 (June 10, 2020), http://doi.org/10.1089/aut.2019.0040.

how would we make a case for an included classroom? How could we explain that the behavior was created by the situation? We need to notice how this can spiral, to understand the situation behind behavior, for the good of all of our students.

During one of Eliza's IEP meetings in first grade, the team asked me about her educational goals. They weren't in the IEP. They weren't written there because her goals were the same as any other kid's goals. The team didn't think that would work. Because she couldn't talk, they didn't know how she could express what she knew. They wanted to put her on modified grades, which meant she would not earn a high school diploma or go to college. It would take away her opportunity for a real academic education. How many students does this happen to every year? How much of a difference can we make when we assume competence and close the expectation gap? Eliza is one example of the expectations we set on students and what happens when we don't assume our students are capable and competent learners.

The expectation gap is real. It happens when we, as educators, create expectations for our students. We do this with the best intentions. We want to set realistic goals and expectations that we know students can meet so they can be successful. But setting a reasonable expectation is too often setting an expectation that is too low. If the goal is easily achieved, we didn't grow or learn as much along the way as we could have.

The expectation gap is more pronounced in our special education students, but it happens with all students. Our kindergarteners are expected to read by the end of the year—what happens when they don't? Are those students thought of as less smart and quick with fewer skills? Do those expectations and ideas follow them through school? Are they being placed in a track for learning, at least in thought, as early as kindergarten? Is learning to read in kindergarten even a reasonable expectation—or one put in place just to have a benchmark? These are all questions we must ask ourselves as educators in our classes, but also as schools and educational systems to see the whole picture.

The first step to moving to a classroom of joyful learners is adjusting our expectations of our students. It means shifting how we look at curriculum and assessment, adjusting how we teach to fit the developmental needs of our students and looking at each student's progress and strengths, meeting them there, and expecting more.

Our old system of learning does not best prepare us for the future of work. We must move from passive students to active learners. We can do that by creating environments for learning. We nurture curiosity and arm students with knowledge about themselves through a culture of social-emotional learning. We assume competency from all students. Then we, as educators, can move from being givers of knowledge to facilitators of real learning.

WHAT DO YOU THINK IS THE BIGGEST CHALLENGE TEACHERS FACE?

"

An archaic system in a new world.

"

—Anonymous seventeen-year veteran teacher

CHAPTER 3

THE BIGGEST CHALLENGE STUDENTS FACE

In the spring of 2020, we were given a gift in the world of education. You think I'm crazy and that this time out of school wasn't a gift, it was a curse, but hear me out. For that moment in time, kids were out of school. There were many issues with equity, engagement, inequalities in quality of education from home, connectivity, technology, and many more. This time glaringly showed the differences in student economic levels, parental support, concentration, and learning differences. We cannot discount those challenges. There is much work to be done.

Let's look past those issues for a moment and focus on the bigger picture of education. We were given a time where all the rules changed. Seat time didn't matter. Standardized tests disappeared; in fact, the California college system eliminated the SAT and ACT for admission. The usual curriculum didn't work from a distance. Educators were given the opportunity to be incredibly creative in the lessons they developed and the ways they delivered them. Students could explore their interests more freely. They had more time to play, learn, and follow their whims. For the first time I can remember, everyone started questioning education and seeking answers.

This time gave us a huge opportunity to explore what is worth teaching and to create new ways of working together within a school. We need to take advantage of this opportunity and do things differently moving forward.

Distance learning was a challenge for my family, like many others. We have two parents working full-time, and two students in elementary school. It took us months to fall into a routine where we could all be productive. But distance learning had its upside. As parents, we were able to spend more time with our children and understand what they were learning in school. My kids had a lot more free time. We were not running from school to after-school activities and sports. We had the gift of time. This gave me the ability to give my kids more freedom and independence. They went for bike rides and walked the dogs around the park and neighborhood. They had time to think of their own projects and creations.

Distance learning versus in-person learning aside, the biggest challenge students face is that the education they receive does not set them up with the skills they need in the real world; their education is not aligned with the skills they need to be successful adults. The biggest challenge education faces is creating learning experiences that teach the knowledge, skills, and concepts that are necessary for success in a changing world. The pandemic has put a spotlight on the misalignment between our current system and necessary future skills. Educators have seen this for years, and now everyone is discussing the same questions and opportunities.

As educators, we can change this by allowing students to follow their interests and facilitating and decoding their personal learning. We need to help them understand and process what they have learned so they can transfer their learning and use it in other aspects of their lives. We need to teach our students how to use technology for networking, education, and connectedness. We need to give them credit for their agency in real-world projects like Mark Metry's Minecraft server and Deborah Olatunji's book, which we'll discuss later in this chapter. Students need an education that sets them up for success through supportive, thoughtful lessons and projects aligned with real-world concepts and skills.

THE SEESAW

One Friday, my eight-year-old daughter announced she wanted to build a seesaw. She sketched her design, found some cardboard, and built a prototype. Her design was good, but I suggested that she do a little research on building seesaws since I guessed others had attempted this before her. She looked around YouTube and found a tutorial and a design she liked made of wood that looked sturdy and easy to make. The guide said it would take one to three hours to build. And the seesaw had padded seats! She studied the tutorial and used it to make a materials list. I double-checked her supply list, and we headed to Home Depot. My daughter has been using simple tools and basic power tools for a while and is familiar with the safety and usefulness of each one. When we got home, she got to work. I let her take the lead and gave her all the tools she should need. I stayed nearby and told her I would help when she needed it. She followed the tutorial, and asked me for help. She would give me directions on what to do—mostly I was just her muscle. She asked me to drill a few screws when she got tired, and asked me to saw a couple of edges (at eight she is not yet allowed to use the power circular saw). She sanded the edges and built the seesaw.

She and her brother now have a super sturdy play toy in our yard whenever they want to seesaw together. Sometimes her dad and I use it, too. But the point of this story is that COVID has given us time to allow our kids and our students to follow their interests and strengths. My daughter loves to create, design, and build things. She was able to understand and use the design process on a project to create a toy she still uses today. If we were in school, she would be learning behind a desk, working on projects with a class, following the group's interests. By working on the seesaw, she learned that she can research, design, create, and build all on her own.

Whether it's on their own or in groups, project-based learning gives our students the skills to take the lead with their learning and create lasting products. Normally, our family would be running to swimming practice, Chinese class, Girl Scouts, or soccer. There wouldn't be time to dig into a personal project. The gift of COVID has been time for our students and children. Without it, we wouldn't have a seesaw.

How can we, as educators, bring these lessons into our classrooms? How can we support students' interests and allow students the time to explore? What will our students create and learn if we let them lead?

When we allow for student agency in the classroom, our students gain skills and confidence. We can do this in a number of ways. It could be through a wonder wall that inspires a student project or choice time in the classroom where students can work on what they desire. It could be by allowing for student discovery on parts of an educator-led project, or creating a whole day each week dedicated to student-led learning. However you choose to create time for student choice in your classroom, it will allow students to develop their interests and use the skills we spend so much time teaching them. Now is the time for students to practice goal setting, trial and error, the design process, the scientific method. The classroom is the space for them to practice using these skills and transferring them to real-world experiences. They need to work on these skills when they are in the classroom and can make mistakes. The process of making mistakes and moving forward continues the learning trajectory and creates lifelong learners. Our students need to master these skills so they can use them in the real world to influence action. We need to be sure they have practiced and mastered their abilities so they understand their strengths and know when to ask for help.

CONNECTEDNESS

The world is changing at an exponential pace. Cars are learning to drive themselves. Surgeries are completed by robots. We can access any information at any time through the internet. Siri and Alexa can answer our questions, text our friends, write our grocery lists, and even order needed items regularly for our homes. We are able to create bots and workflows to run our business communications and request almost anything for delivery without leaving our homes (which has been handy during the COVID-19 pandemic). All of these tools are automated and create more time for the people using them. They are also run and created by people. With an education system that hasn't changed in over one hundred years but a society that is forcing new ways of thinking, education is like a Ford Model T on the freeway. We need to give our kids the resources, skills, and information they need to be successful in this rapidly changing world.

So, what does that look like? Does that mean that all students should be learning to code and program, or should all students learn entrepreneurship skills? Some have said that the world is being split into two groups of people: those who can code and those who can't. That doesn't mean that we need to teach everyone coding, but those students who have at least a basic understanding of coding and programming will have an advantage as they work with programmers and designers to create and innovate. Those who can't code will need to be creative and persuasive to make their ideas and dreams come to fruition.

We also need to be creative and persuasive when we talk about ourselves, our accomplishments, our beliefs, and our vision on the internet. We are in a world of constant connectedness, where building our online brand is almost as important as what we actually do in the world around us. Currently, these platforms include LinkedIn, Instagram, TikTok and Clubhouse, Facebook and Twitter. I'm sure they will change, but it is important that we teach students how to create their online brand, as well as how to have the social-emotional skills to understand the difference between online branding and actual human behavior.

When I look on LinkedIn, I see few educators who are active and engaged. Yet this is the world our students will need to navigate to network, find opportunities, and work together. Platforms like this have given us access to more people in more levels of business than ever before. With a general belief that most people want to help and will support those who ask, this ability to instantly connect with CEOs, founders, and executives is unprecedented. As educators, we need to teach the skills to connect online as well as the etiquette and ethics of online communities. This is an important skill in the changing world and a challenge that schools need to recognize.

To show how social media and online branding have changed the workforce, I'll share a story from when I began working in, well, let's just call it the mid-90s. When I wanted to change jobs and land a position in a new industry or at a specific company, I first had to call the company. There would be a main phone line and a receptionist to answer it. I'd ask for someone in human resources. Usually I'd get transferred to someone, and then I had a name that I could reach out to (now you can search for someone on LinkedIn and request a connection). It usually wasn't the right person, and often that person wouldn't return my call. I would keep calling, and my persistence paid off (this is still true; persistence pays off, and it is a trait we should be teaching). Eventually, my new contact would either call back or answer the phone and direct me toward the right person. This could take days, weeks, or even months. This didn't mean I got a job—this meant I had an opportunity to talk with the right person and now I knew where to send my résumé. Let's fast forward to 2001. I wanted to work for an advertising agency. I needed to look them up in the yellow pages (remember those?) and find all the local agencies and their addresses. I took my résumé door to door, hoping to talk to someone or at least make an impression that would get it into the right hands.

All of this has changed. We don't use the yellow pages, we don't go door to door with résumés, and we can't even call the main line of an organization because it often doesn't exist. Many of our schools are not teaching students the skills needed to navigate the world of social media, online portfolios, and personal branding, even though these are the new rules and norms of communication. Instead, students figure them out on their own, learning from peers or finding mentors. If they learn these skills in school, we can help them succeed. How can we help them to be safe? We can include aspects of safe and useful internet knowledge when we build projects. We can incorporate personal branding into writing assignments. As creative and innovative educators, we can figure out imaginative ways to teach these skills.

We can use this instant access to people we want to know for so many different things. In March 2020, I decided to interview leaders in education to amplify voices, share thoughts, and become part of the conversation on what is happening in education. I wanted to hear how our thought leaders believed we could make significant changes in education. I reached out to authors whose books I had read, CEO's I followed, educators and students, and asked for thirty minutes of their time. Overwhelmingly, they agreed to the conversations. This project is now the Rebel Educator Podcast, but what is important in this example is that these opportunities are available to our students every day.

We can do this in our schools as well. At UP Academy, we have reached out to virtual speakers, people who we normally wouldn't have access to because of travel and time constraints. Now Zoom meetings are normal, and most people are willing to give thirty minutes to educating kids. This has huge implications for education, as experts are now easily accessible.

As educators, we need to give students the skills to create these connections and networks and know what to say when they reach the right person. We need to model it in our classrooms and in our lives. We need to help students see the possibilities of the world around them.

This starts in elementary school, where our goal is to lay a solid foundation for students to build upon. We need to give them a wide variety of experiences and knowledge so they can begin to understand where their interests and strengths interconnect. We help students see what their superpowers are.

Students work on communication skills when they make presentations. Starting in kindergarten, they should be learning how to address a group of people. They need to work on cross-curricular projects that help them understand how different pieces in the puzzle of the world fit together. We work on these skills in school so they can piece them together on their own later.

IMPLICATIONS FOR STUDENTS WITH DISABILITIES

Access to a network, the ability to communicate effectively online and in person, and the ability to understand coding all have huge implications for those students who are disadvantaged or have disabilities. When all of our students, in all of our schools, are learning relevant, project-based material, when they are learning how to speak in front of people and effectively share their ideas and their work, and when all of our students have the basic skills to make their dreams come to fruition—at least online—we will have come a long way toward equity.

When we talk about the achievement gap, these skills are part of the reason for its existence. Students from more advantaged families gain networking and communication skills at home. I have asked my kids since they were three to give me a three-pronged argument for why they should get a toy, or a Popsicle, or stay up late to watch a movie. They have to determine the benefits of the desired outcome and how to convey those to me in a persuasive way to get what they want. These weren't skills I was taught when I was growing up living on food stamps and hoping our next social security check would pay the rent and the phone bill. These aren't skills our schools teach, but they are necessary in the world. What if schools did teach *and* give students the technical coding and communication skills they need to get ahead in a world built on technology? What would it mean for our students from different backgrounds to get an equal education?

When I think of my daughter Eliza and everything the world held for her, I remember being both terrified and excited. As a person with a disability, there was so much cruelty and so much that could have been inaccessible to her. There was also so much hope. In 2015, I attended a conference on neuro gaming and was amazed by the possibilities. Companies working to create communication using brainwaves. For my daughter with cerebral palsy, that would mean not having to control her body to hit keys on a keyboard or trying to control her head to activate an eye gaze machine. It would give her the ability to think of words and watch them appear on a screen. Almost real-time communication! And the ability to be a doctor through using her thoughts (surgery by robot), or a writer, researcher, or lawyer. It would open so many doors for her and others with disabilities, as long as our schools could provide an education that included these skills for everyone.

For a student with disabilities like Eliza, it becomes imperative to have access to the full academic curriculum. It is important to be included in mainstream classroom learning. It was important that Eliza's teachers find ways to ensure that she, and other students with challenges, can reach their full potential. Students need all of this knowledge and these skills to take advantage of what technology makes possible. Without an education, our students with and without disabilities cannot network, access the knowledge and connections of others, or dream of becoming a surgeon or software developer.

Collaborating with peers on project-based material in school means students can fully participate in their learning. It opens doors of opportunity where there weren't any before. It begins to level the playing field for students who do not have all the advantages.

When we utilize project-based learning, it means that every student can participate in each project in their own way. It includes students of all abilities and builds on students' strengths while supporting their weaknesses. When students in Eliza's class got the opportunity to choose their groups, they always chose to work with her. She excelled at big-picture thinking, helping to resolve conflicts, and making choices. These attributes all contribute to being a great teammate. For students with dyslexia, they can contribute ideas without having to write everything down. For students with attention challenges, projects often naturally mitigate the issues as they are expected to ask questions, move around the classroom, and interact with the material and each other. Project-based learning opens up opportunities for students to work together and learn from each other. It allows each student to feel fully part of the class.

There are so many ways we can look to technology to change the future. For people who are unable to drive due to motor disabilities, loss of limbs, or lack of sight, autonomous driving cars open up a whole new world. Now, people with disabilities have to hire a driver or rely on public transportation, but soon they will be able to get in a car, program a location on the vehicle's computer, and go. One of the first engineerless test drives of Waymo, Google's self-driving car company, was by a blind man who was astounded by the possibilities it opened up for him. So much in the world is rapidly changing, and if our educational system can keep up, there are new possibilities for everyone.

TECHNOLOGY IS NOT HUMANITY

Anyone who has participated in Zoom meetings all day, then Zoom happy hour in an attempt to have social time with other humans knows it is hard to connect with a cold, flat screen, even if there is a smiling face in the box. The question for technology becomes not one of how do we use it to make our lives richer, but how do we share our feelings and our humanity through technology? How do we make technology empathetic? Companies like Jibo and Affectiva are working on solutions to make artificial intelligence and technology more empathetic and ethical, but these are also questions our children will face as they enter the workforce.

We teach social-emotional learning and effective communication in school to support students' understanding of themselves and others. This is often taught through one class, one hour a week or even one hour a month. We leave a lot of this teaching to the parents, and as long as students behave in class, we often don't explore deeper. Students also learn empathy through the humanities, history, social studies, and social justice. For educators, there is a huge opportunity to connect the Social Emotional Learning (SEL) lessons with the lessons we learn from the humanities. We must ensure these subjects have equal focus in our projects and curriculum as the STEAM (science, technology, engineering, art, and math) subjects currently enjoy. Art, music, movement, and mindfulness help build the base for empathetic action and understanding in our students.

When we allow ample time for projects and exploration around the issues that have faced humanity, we can dive deep into the human relationships and interconnectedness that have brought about conflict or peace. We can give students a better understanding of how the world works as a whole. We can see the relationships of how groups interact together and make both good and bad decisions. It's through studying the past that we can provide our students with knowledge that helps them understand the world around them and be thoughtful in their actions. We can study their mistakes and choices. We can understand what brings about conflict and what brings together community. When we teach only science and STEM skills, our students learn a process and a method. When we add the humanities and social sciences, they learn how those processes and methods affect society. Both of these are important as we continue to rebuild and refresh our planet. In fact, they may be imperative if we are to save humanity.

From an educational perspective, this all starts with how we build relationships with our students and help them connect concepts with experiences that allow for deeper learning. They need to master their core subjects, but more importantly, they need to understand the problems in the world they can work to solve. From a young age, students need to be focused on how they can influence action in the world around them with the skills and knowledge they are learning in school. As educators we create ecosystems of learning for our students that incorporate local, national, or global problems and the professionals and leaders working to solve them. When we bring these issues to students and have them work together with influencers in a meaningful way, we begin to do what we set out to do as educators. We begin to change the world.

Life skills classes like cooking, gardening, woodworking, sewing, building, and art all contribute to building a broad base of knowledge and understanding of how the world works. These experiences help build solutions-minded, flexible, and creative thinking for innovation. Elementary school education should provide this broad base of knowledge and experience for students to grow from. We need to teach students skills to manage themselves in the world. We need to provide a sample of the vast variety of interests to be explored. This is the time for them to discover what they like and don't like as well as where their strengths and weaknesses lie. Students begin this work in elementary school and continue to refine their strengths and recognize their challenges as they move through middle and high school. We need to be there to provide encouragement, support, and real-world knowledge so our students can be capable citizens when they move on from our classes. Students need a solid foundation of knowledge to build on and grow. Educators can provide this through creating immersive project experiences that challenge their students.

GIVE CREDIT FOR WORLD-CHANGING WORK

The biggest challenge students face is that their education is not aligned with the skills they need to be successful adults. Many of our schools have not shifted to help students become future ready. The future holds a new world, where many current jobs will be done by robots, and technology will assist us in almost everything we do. The future includes programming ethical decision-making for artificial intelligence and requires the emotional intelligence and foresight to understand the implications of this. It includes a world where we will all be more connected online and will need to work to ensure we also stay connected as humans. Education needs to shift to support the characteristics our students will need to be successful. It needs to recognize achievement in all its variations. It's time to see past the letter placed on the top of a test.

One outspoken example of this is Mark Metry. Mark is the bestselling author of *Screw Being Shy* and the host of a global top 100 podcast, *Humans 2.0*. In 2009, he almost failed out of school. He was bored, didn't feel he was learning anything relevant, and as a member of an immigrant family, he was different from other students at his school. The social structure had failed him. Other students treated him poorly; they were racist and mean. Mark started doing projects in his spare time that were relevant and meaningful to him. He had a few failures until he followed his interest in playing the video game

Minecraft and launched a player-owned Minecraft server that became number 1 and reached over 10 million users. He didn't get any credit for this project in high school and was still failing his classes. He was doing poorly in the game of school, but beginning to win at the game of life. Mark managed to finish high school, and the successes kept coming. Mark was a mix of persistent and lucky, but it came with a cost. He spent years grappling with obesity, depression, and social anxiety, searching for self-worth and meaning in the world. The message he heard from school was one of failure, and he carried this with him for a long time. He pulled himself up, but what about all the others that education fails in this way? Many young adults don't have the support system or mental strength to get through it. What about all the students the system fails, the world losing their voices and their potential in the process? These are not dumb or bad kids; they just didn't work well with the institutionalized system of learning.

In Mark's case, he accomplished many things in high school and beyond, not *because* of high school but *in spite* of high school. What might his world have looked like if his teachers had supported his success instead of demanding he meet their definitions of success? Maybe he could have been spared years of ill health and self-doubt. How many other students experience the same thing? Mark's story shows us it's time to change the way we educate. It's not a one-size-fits-all box. Instead, there needs to be a box for every size, with a way to give students credit for their real-world efforts and ingenuity.

Deborah Olatunji is another student who excelled in life, but did not get credit in school for all her achievements. Deborah did well in school, juggling her outside interests and academic courses. She saw that not all students had that capacity and thought there was a better way. She started an innovation club at her high school to support her fellow peers in personal development, self-exploration, and entrepreneurship to help them build their capacity. While still in high school, she began working to redesign high school and wrote a book describing her vision. In this book, *Unleashing Your Innovative Genius: High School Redesigned* (for which she received no high school credit), she interviewed and centered the voices of students, teachers, parents, and mentors alongside her own stories to uncover actionable ways to make education exciting and purposeful for her generation. As she began her college journey, she launched a podcast, *Voices of Disruption*, where she continues this movement to learn from others, grow and reflect on her life, pursue what she's interested in, and cheer people on as they define success on their own terms, not the terms defined by an educator, a school, or a system.

While Deborah was writing her book, she still had to keep up her junior and senior English classes. She wrote a book, but did not get credit for it in her English classes. Writing a book is a journey that lets students learn about something they care about and want to change. It takes more time, heart, and dedication than course-work. Why are we not allowing students to design some of their own learning experiences? Why aren't we creating the space for these ideas and explorations to grow in school?

The past reasoning of needing to be in school for a certain number of hours or needing to fulfill college requirements is quickly going by the wayside. We know we don't learn by the number of hours we spend in a seat at a desk; rather, we learn by the experiences we have. Educators and districts need to work together to realign what we need to know with what we actually do in class. This starts with identifying what is important for the student to leave knowing. What does a successful graduate look like? When we know the kind of students we want to release into the world, it becomes easier to change the educational system to produce those students.

Educators need to support students' challenges but also challenge students' strengths. The coming decades will lead to some of the biggest questions we've faced as a species in history. The next generation will face questions of morality, humanity, and innovation in technology like no other before it. They will need to shape empathetic and ethically moral artificial intelligence, stop climate change, and manage the impending energy crisis. They will also need to stop social media, data mining, and the news media from warping our perceived reality. Their responses will shape the face of the planet. The biggest challenge students face is that the education they receive does not set them up with the skills they need in the real world. How are we as educators preparing them to make these decisions?

WHAT IS YOUR BEST MOMENT TEACHING?

"

We did a 'throwaway' lesson one year because we had extra time after the state tests. I say 'throwaway' because it was based on NO standards for my class. I had my seventh graders research a career they wanted; it had to be a 'real career' (no reality TV stars, etc.). They had to research how much they would get paid, the outlook for that career, what type of education, all that. I had them backward plan, and had them make a plan all the way to the high school in our area that would lead them to their best outlook. (We were in an area with many magnet high schools.) About seven years later, I had a mom in the after-school pickup line tell me that her son made that plan, stuck to it, and was accepted into MIT.

"

—Courtney, veteran teacher of fourteen years

CHAPTER 4

WHAT IS THE PURPOSE OF YOUR LESSON?

In my survey of educators, I asked what was the biggest frustration of teaching. Most of them mentioned teaching to the test, following a curriculum map, or having to "get through" the curriculum. They talked about wanting to teach to the class, not the test, to plan lessons around relevant material and current events, not canned curriculum. They desired the leeway to design lessons around the class's areas of interest and more time for exploration. If you are reading this as an educator, you may have these same frustrations.

As we look at our educational system, it leads us to question why we are teaching this way. What do we really want our students to learn, and how can we best support that? Educators know that one of the best ways to learn is through modeling behavior. As such, we need to allow our teachers the same agency we want them to lead our students to discover.

During the pandemic, I began an interview series of thought leaders. This was first released on YouTube as *Voices of Education* and more recently as the *Rebel Educator* podcast. I wanted to amplify the voices of those leading the efforts to change education and also offer a chance to be heard to students and educators working in the system. Several major themes emerged as we discussed how our educational system could change for the better:

- Stop rote memorization for the test and instead focus on what concepts are behind the content.

- Listen to our students and ask them what they would like to learn.

- Respect our students' capacity and capability as learners and work to be learning engineers or coaches instead of preachers of information.

- Trust the creativity and professionalism of our educators.

- Support the development of mature emotional intelligence in our educators.

In our discussions about what and how to teach, the issue of memorizing state capitals is often used as an example. This lesson is still widely taught in the third or fourth grade in the United States. Students are asked to learn all fifty states and memorize their capitals. What is the purpose of this lesson? Are we teaching memorization, history, or facts? Why do students need to know this information? I recently saw a Facebook post from a distance learning parent looking for resources to teach this content. Out of curiosity, I asked why she was teaching it. Her answer? "Because it is part of the curriculum." We all know it is, but *why* are we still teaching it? Is learning the state names and capitals really the needed information in the lesson?

It is important to know the states and basic geography of the United States as a United States citizen. It aids in understanding our history and how the state and federal governments work together and against each other in our democracy. It is also important to understand how state governments work and what the capital of each state signifies. Maybe we add the history of the capital in your state, how it came to be in that location, and whether it was built by enslaved or contracted workers. We could then analyze what this means for the past and future of the state's social constructs. All of this leads us to question what role the government plays in our lives.

Information that can be quickly accessed by asking, "Hey Google," like what is the capital of Wyoming, does not require a learning engineer. Rather, deeper learning around the role government plays in our lives and how state, federal, and global governments interact are the nuanced topics that require a human to explain and explore the humanity and ethics of government types and styles.

Getting an A for knowing that Cheyenne is the capital of Wyoming (which I just googled and I'm sure I had this lesson in elementary school and likely got an A) is not useful or helpful in the future of life. Learning the history of the struggle and conflict between the government and the Cheyenne people and how that influences state government today in Wyoming is nuanced, challenging, and useful. Now the lesson teaches us about capitals but also about conflict and indigenous peoples' rights, as well as our own government's role in taking over the land.

As educators, we should spend time teaching what students need us to teach—the nuances, connections, and historical significance from multiple points of view. If students can ask Siri, they don't need us to teach it; and by doing so, we are underutilizing our skills and knowledge as educators. To make the biggest impact, we must share the best of our skills, and that probably isn't memorizing facts. If our job as educators is to prepare our students for the world of tomorrow, we need to be giving them the skills and tools that will be useful in multiple situations, like understanding conflict and resolution, not just answering questions on a multiple-choice test. Every lesson should start with that purpose in mind.

LISTEN TO YOUR STUDENTS

We need to ask our students what is interesting and important to them. Then we can create engaging material to help them understand the roles and opportunities the future holds and support their learning.

I'd like to share another story from Professor Sheckley, because he has so many amazing ones. He tells a story of an educator who was teaching the Revolutionary War. There was nothing special in the way this educator taught the material—the students learned battles, generals, and dates. Two girls in the class noticed that all the generals and soldiers were men. They wondered, "Where were the women?" Their teacher allowed them to explore that question and discover what the role of women was in the war and during wartime. In cooperation with the librarian, their teacher set up resources on the school's media website for the girls to explore. As the teacher and the librarian found more references, they set up links to access this information. The students were learning how to use the teacher as a resource to advance their learning—a key skill of agency—and not see her as the sole fountain for their learning. The girls were able to use their agency as learners to take advantage of resources in their environment to advance their understanding. These girls had the opportunity to understand aspects of the war that others in their class didn't. They got to follow their interests. They did the work, understood the war, did research, wrote a paper, and were fully engaged in their perspective because they found it interesting. They were able to use the resources that were made available to them effectively. I bet they remember this information and can still speak intelligently about women's roles in the Revolutionary War. I'd also bet none of the other students in that class remember the names of the battles or dates they needed to pass a test.

As educators, we can encourage our students to explore interests within a topic from a young age. For example, at UP Academy, we chose space as our first full school theme last year. Everyone learned basic information about the solar system, the sun, and the universe; then each student chose something to focus on. The topics ranged from the sun to Ganymede, a moon of Jupiter. Each child was engaged in their research because they had chosen a topic that interested them.

One of the greatest examples of students being engaged in project-based learning is in the movie *Bill and Ted's Excellent Adventure*. Bored by their lessons, failing their history class, and skipping too much school, Bill and Ted must pass their history report to stay in school. Fortunately, they find help from a man named Rufus, who has a time machine. Bill and Ted proceed to explore time and space. They experience different time periods, meet the people they are learning about, and bring them back to the future for their class report. These historical figures share their contributions to the world with the class. Spoiler alert: Bill and Ted pass history and graduate. While we may not all be able to travel through time and space, we can create these kinds of experiences through drama, sewing, and costuming. We can support our students' research and writing and help them develop an understanding of the concepts that have shaped our world.

As educators, when we move from allowing some students, usually the high-achieving ones, to stray from the core curriculum, and instead make the concept and the "straying" the core of the curriculum, students become empowered to use their strengths and take control of their learning. They begin to understand that their interest, curiosity, and ideas are important. They also become much more engaged in the process and produce better work with higher craftsmanship. When I interviewed teachers, overwhelmingly they said that their jobs were better when students were excited about the content. One way to ensure this is to teach to the student—ask them what they want to learn.

ASSESSING PROJECT-BASED LEARNING AND STANDARDIZED TESTS

Assessment becomes a question when our learning becomes more abstract. In project-based learning, we focus more on the process than the product, on the learning journey rather than the answers to a test. We may have students working on different projects at different times. Educators teaching in different systems consistently ask how we can assess learning and skills. Most educators structure a class so students learn information, then share it with the teacher on a test. But are tests the most accurate measure of performance? As students leave high school, and definitely as they leave college, they have portfolios of work, websites, references, and loads of information that show how they took what they learned in the classroom and applied it to a real project, internship, or job. Assessments need to move from how to regurgitate knowledge to get an A on a test to measuring what a student has learned and how they have improved over time. If we want to produce good learners who can take knowledge and apply it in the world, this idea of improvement over time is the best scale of assessment.

Self-assessment is also important. When we ask students what they want to learn, we must also ask them how they will judge their learning. As adults, we often do this without formal assessment or even thinking about it. We self-assess our tasks daily. For example, when straightening up the kitchen, we ask ourselves, *Is the sink clean?* Maybe a couple of dishes are in the sink, but the dishwasher is full; maybe there is food stuck to the sides. We assess and decide whether it is clean enough and move on. But if we were staging the house for sale, the answer to the assessment would be, *No, it needs further cleaning.* We look and think, *It's not perfect, but it's good enough for now.* If you were being graded, would you get an A today in sink cleaning? Maybe not, but every project is not about getting an A. Sometimes "good enough for now" is good enough. How are we teaching students to use their judgment? Some projects are about the process, and some are about finishing it "good enough" to go on to the next thing. Some parts of the project need to be exact, and some just need to be finished. Some projects are the day you are trying to sell the house, and some are not. Allowing students to decide which projects are the priority, which need to be finished until good enough, and which need to be revised until a desired outcome is an important life skill. It may not be important to keep your sink spotless every day, but it is important to double-check the load levels of a building you are constructing. *What needs to be an 'A,' and what just needs to be done?* Self-assessment and judgment is important.

We are in an interesting time because, as I write this, standardized tests have been cancelled for the remainder of the year. The University of California system has decided that SAT and ACT tests will not be needed for incoming freshmen until at least 2024. Shelter-in-place restrictions have closed schools and eliminated the current "seat time" requirements. Educators have a chance to reimagine what their classrooms look like, and administrators have a chance to support creativity and flexibility in learning. Time will tell what changes will result from this time, as many children have thrived at home, while others have struggled. We all agree that magic happens in the classroom. Hopefully, this opportunity will give our educators a chance to be the magicians they envisioned when they began the journey of teaching.

How we use assessments matters for how we evaluate ourselves as educators as well as how we judge students' learning. We teach with a project- and concept-based curriculum that we often create as we go. We can use assessments to find holes in student mastery and see where we need to add material in our next projects or curriculum. Assessing students on content and moving on without covering the missed material does not help them gain confidence or mastery. When we use the assessment as a gauge and review or move forward with material, we can be sure our students are truly learning what we want to help them understand.

Students learn deeper, retain information better, and are able to transfer that knowledge to other areas when they understand the underlying concepts. They are more engaged and interested when the learning is relevant. The ability to transfer knowledge—to use and apply information to other areas of life—is the true goal of education.

USING LESSONS IN THE WORLD

We don't live our lives by tests and answers, scores or grades. Rather, we live our lives by continuing to learn. We make decisions utilizing the skills and experience we acquire. How can we equip our students to make the best decisions possible? How can we help them to transfer the information they learn in school and apply it to the world around them? Our job as educators is to help students develop these skills.

This information and these skills should be the same. The skills inside the walls of school should be the same as the ones out in the big world. If no one has asked you for the capital of Idaho since fifth grade, and given you a job, a paycheck, or even a pat on the back for having the right answer, maybe this is not the important stuff we need to be teaching. (In case you are curious, it is

Boise; I googled that, too.) Content is everywhere—how we learn to use it and understand the concepts behind it will make a difference in the education and lives of our students.

When we understand what the true purpose of our lesson is, we can teach from a new perspective. We must dig below the surface of the content and the curriculum and really understand what we want our students to gain. We need to know what they need to learn. More importantly, we need to understand what they will be able to do with the knowledge once they have it. If the goal is to know the dates and battles of the Revolutionary War to get a good grade on a test, then reciting dates might be enough. If the goal is to understand how war develops from conflict, what causes conflict, the systems and roles in society affected by war, and ways of resolving conflict before war, perhaps we want to teach from a different angle. I would prefer to avoid the war than be left memorizing the dates of the battles.

WHAT IS YOUR BEST MOMENT TEACHING?

"

Watching the excitement a child has when he/she learns a skill or grasps a new concept (the light bulb moment). Watching children take ownership and pride in their learning.

"

—Jennifer, twenty-three-year veteran teacher

CHAPTER 5

ENGAGING ALL LEARNERS

MY STEAM SEMESTER

During UP Academy's first year of operation, I had the opportunity to teach a semester of math and science, two big components of STEAM. I started the class by asking my second graders what they wanted to learn that term. The answers I received ranged from penguins and seals and tree frogs to creating a desk. As an educator, I stepped back and took a look at their upcoming math units, the NGSS (Next Generation Science Standards) and the supplies we had to work with. I then built a couple of projects that would incorporate all of these things.

First we worked on our wood project. As a small, new school without a wood shop or a great deal of outdoor space, building full-size desks with seven-year-olds was not possible. But, learning the size of a desk, practicing measurements, understanding fractions through building a smaller scale model, drawing out the 2D sides needed to piece together a 3D object, were possible. I wrote the project to incorporate elements of math, engineering, and art, and we set out to create 1/3 scale objects of what we wanted to create. One student chose a dog house (which was challenging with lots of sides and pieces), and another chose a table (much easier—only five pieces). The students then learned to use yard sticks, meter sticks, centimeters, and inches as we learned the general sizes of things in the world around us. They spent a day running around and measuring everything they could find in the school. Then we decided what size our objects should be, rounded those measurements (estimation), and split them in thirds (fractions) to create the sizes we would build. They drew them out on graph paper (art), each 2D side (2D to 3D math concept), cut them from wood, and pieced them together (engineering).

We also learned about ecosystems and biomes. We started by going into our schoolyard and looking at a six-inch square of yard and understanding the ecosystem of that spot. Then we looked at the larger landscape around us and discussed the ecosystem of the Santa Cruz mountains. We studied the bigger picture of biomes and the global water system. We took field trips to the zoo to learn about habitats and to the air museum to learn about weather and the water system. We built mountains from cornmeal and learned about erosion and canyon formation when it rained. We planted seeds in light, in dark, and in water to see what would happen. We talked about rainforests, the Arctic, and the oceans. Students researched using books and the internet to find the creatures they wanted to learn more about. They built their own biomes using soil, worms, water, water plants, and seeds. They chose an animal and learned about its habitat, ecosystem, and biome and created a vision of it in their own creative way. Some created a diorama of their biome, and others built their animal out of clay and created a habitat out of cardboard and paper. Students followed their interests, were engaged in learning, and covered the standards that had been laid out for them to learn.

But perhaps the best part of this semester wasn't the projects—it was how we used our time. We turned the afternoon into Flexible Learning Time. Since this was elementary school, we still needed to cover basic math lessons and concepts outside of measurement, 2D/3D, and graphing. Each Monday I would lay out the work we needed to complete that week, and each day the students would discuss and decide what they wanted to work on. Some days they were in the mood to write, and some days they wanted to build. Students should have a say about what they work on. It allows them to be more deeply engaged, hold their attention longer, and follow the natural rhythms of their thoughts and feelings. These are all important goals of education and growing up.

THE QUESTIONS OF EDUCATION

As we move beyond Common Core, or at least look for new and interesting ways to teach it, we need to ask a few key questions:

- What lessons are we teaching?

- What is important to learn?

- What concepts, skills, and knowledge are needed to build a base for succeeding in the world around us?

These questions can be asked at the beginning of each year, month, and lesson as we strive to create the best environment for our students. It also supports us as educators. As we look back to why educators leave the profession, it is often because of a lack of creativity in the job and classroom. Educators stay because they love seeing the joy of learning in their students' eyes. Educators need to be empowered to use their brilliance to stoke the fires of wonder each day. Kids are incredible, and teaching them should be full of exploration, joy, and fun.

MAKING PROJECT-BASED LEARNING INCLUSIVE

When I first started learning about project-based learning, I couldn't see how it would adapt to all students. It felt impossible to engage students with attention issues, students who had difficulty connecting and working with others, and students with limited physical abilities on one project.

I've heard this is a sentiment from other educators as well. There is a misconception that project-based learning is only for the "bright" or gifted kids. They worry that students with challenges will not be able to manage their time, bodies, or minds to follow through on project work.

There are three major flaws with this limiting thinking:

1. Everyone does small (or large) projects every day. Almost everything we do in our personal and professional lives is made up of little projects. Think back to the kitchen sink example. We can help students identify what needs to be done, understand how to do it, and assess if it was done appropriately through project-based learning in our classrooms.

2. Everyone needs space and time to find their limits and overcome their challenges. Even gifted students, sometimes especially gifted students, struggle to accurately and gracefully self-assess. By allowing students agency in their projects, each student will naturally scaffold to their abilities. By allowing them to do some self-assessment, we can look at progress in the process but also in their perception of the outcomes over time.

3. The expectation gap this thinking propagates. This is the difference between what we think is possible for our kids and what they are capable of achieving. It says we expect our gifted students

to excel at project learning, but what expectation does that put on everyone else?

I saw the expectation gap firsthand and with the clarity of a magnifying glass with Eliza, my daughter with cerebral palsy. She was capable of so many things, but limited by how those around her were willing to engage her and what opportunities they were willing to give her. When we limit project-based learning to only the "bright" kids, we place the same limitations on all children we have decided are not "bright." We are throwing kids into the expectation-gap chasm. We are deciding what our students are capable of and what type of education they will receive. Instead, we should provide a framework and structure for learners to show us what they are capable of. The future of education is to create a space where all students can thrive, regardless of their "track," giftedness, or status. All students have amazing ideas, imagination, and possibility. It is our job as educators not to limit their potential by what we think they can accomplish; instead, we need to give them a foundation and a platform from which to jump and show us how high they can soar.

Progress over time is the real measurement of learning. Students pay more attention when they are engaged, and they work better together when they are invested in the end goal. Sometimes students can work on a solo project and discover the value in learning all the parts of a project and putting together the pieces on their own. Other times students can collaborate and each bring their strengths to contribute to a larger outcome. Students can be assigned parts of a project that speak to their weaknesses so they can face their challenges successfully. Sometimes they can be assigned to their strengths so they can lead and teach others. As educators, the art of crafting lessons is to give each student the right challenge at the right time.

Students with physical disabilities can play all of those roles and within a group have the opportunity to provide input and guidance. A group setting may also mean that they may not need to physically build anything themselves. They can share their ideas on where pieces go, how to create, or their vision for the project. The students who are able bodied can make it happen. This allows a student with disabilities to become a director, problem solver, and leader of the project. In a typical class, this student might be left behind or asked to do something that is not appropriate for their abilities. More likely, they may not be involved in the class at all. Project-based learning is inclusive by nature, and when we use it to bring the right challenges to each of our students, it builds the self-esteem and self-worth of all of our students.

FITTING IN INQUIRY AND CONCEPT LEARNING

We've talked about how project-based learning and flexible learning times can work to allow students to have independent choice. But what about teaching concepts or inquiry-based learning, and how might those fit into the framework of a school day?

The Wonder Wall

The wonder wall idea comes from the work of Harvey "Smokey" Daniels, a classroom teacher, college professor, and author of *The Curious Classroom*. I believe it to be one of the easiest and fastest ways to build engagement and reignite a sense of wonder in a classroom. It has the added benefits of being easy to implement, not taking a lot of time, and drawing excitement from the students. A wonder wall consists of a bulletin board, white board, or board of Post-it notes—whatever you have available. Its magic is that it is always accessible to students. The wonder wall may need to be modeled for a few weeks before all the students get into it, but when they do, you will glean an overwhelming amount of information from them as they begin to imagine and learn.

The wonder wall sits in the classroom as a place where students can put any question they have about the world. (Depending on the age of students, some reminders about appropriateness may be necessary.) It relies on mutual respect: no one writes on another person's questions, and no one takes down anyone's questions. If others have the same questions or thoughts, you add stars or checks next to those questions. Students can add to the wall anytime during the week. Questions I've received on UP Academy's wonder walls include, "How do cars work?" "Why is the sun yellow?" "Why do white police kill Black people?" You need to be prepared for anything.

The wonder wall is a gateway to becoming a coach for learning. It can be a first step to broadening a classroom or an addition to a classroom already full of agency. Sometimes student questions are answered simply and only take a few moments, like "Why do dogs bark?" Or you may want to dig deeper and ask more questions, like: What are dogs' expressions? What do different barks sound like? Can dogs talk to each other? Wonder wall questions may turn into a small class project all on their own. The question about dogs could prompt the class to explore creative, narrative, or persuasive writing, video development, or field trips to the Humane Society or to see a veterinarian. There are so many exciting things that could come from a simple question. It may be a small side project for a few students, or a few different groups could work on different questions. It could turn into a full class project exploring communication styles and companionship.

It's easy to see how the inquiry of a student could grow into a project. But to get started, we only need to create the wall and invite student questions.Not all students will have questions every week and participation is not required, which is good because a class of twenty to thirty kids could generate hundreds of questions a week with an inquisitive group. We also need to make time to address the questions. This can be done by spending thirty minutes a week looking at, answering, and discussing questions, or watching videos that explain them. We can do research and use the internet to explore topics we are not knowledgeable about. Going through these exercises with students helps them develop skills for life-long learning. It helps them understand how to find reputable sources to answer their most burning questions. They also see that their teacher is constantly learning, which models lifelong learning for students. It drives excitement, experimentation, and curiosity in the class as each student waits for their questions to be answered.

I urge you to start a wonder wall and think of it as an experiment and use a growth mindset surrounding the outcome. See what happens when you ask students to share their questions and you as an educator begin to lead them down paths of discovery.

The Coachineal Project

In my daughter Eliza's kindergarten year, her teacher, Ms. Bonnie, got a scarf dyed from little insects called coachineals. Ms. Bonnie told her class about the scarf and how it was made, and the students wondered if they could dye fabric that way, too. Never one to shy away from a project or learning opportunity, Ms. Bonnie said they should try.

The students got coachineals to see what they looked like and the dye itself to learn how it was made. Here's where the project got interesting. Every year the school had a market day where each class created a "product" and "sold" it to all the students. The currency: beads. Each student received ten beads to "buy" products from other classes. Each student was also required to "work" a shift in their own class store. The students were deciding what to "sell" that year. The best products were ones that shoppers could interact with and make themselves. The class decided to make cochineal shrinky dink charms. Each customer colored their own cochineal and adult volunteers shrank them. The class made string colored with cochineal dye to hang the shrinky dink charms. Each customer received a personal cochineal shrinky dink necklace with cochineal dyed string as the chain. Ms. Bonnie incorporated art, entrepreneurship, history, and culture into a lesson that began with a scarf and followed students' interests to end with almost every student in the school having their own cochineal dyed necklace—with a charm picturing a cochineal!

STUDENT AGENCY

We give students agency by asking them what they want to learn and when they want to learn it. When we include students in the planning of our time and lessons, we tell them that we respect their choices and that they are capable learners. We build their confidence with the message that their ideas and interests are important enough to spend time on. We show them how to be successful in their own learning. In contrast, when we ask them to sit and listen, we praise them for following directions, not thinking independently. Do we want our future workers and colleagues to only do what we ask them to do? Or do we want them to think of new solutions, ask thought-provoking questions, and collaborate to create new innovations?

When we respect students' interests and choice in learning, we create a subtle but large shift in building self-esteem. We teach them the ability to trust their thoughts and ideas. Allowing them to choose uses their strengths while engaging more students and making lessons more inclusive. How can we, as educators, give our students more free choice in our lessons, projects, and classes?

WHY DID YOU BECOME A TEACHER?

> "
> It brings me joy to help others grow in their abilities and foster curiosity in the world.
> "

—Whitney DeBordenave,
eleven-year veteran educator

CHAPTER 6

SKILLS, CONCEPTS, AND KNOWLEDGE

THE IDENTITY PROJECT

Identity is a concept we learn throughout our lives. We constantly shape and form parts of our identity, while other pieces, like who our parents are and where we were born, are static. We learn to share our identity through effective communication skills and emotional intelligence. A deep understanding of ourselves is necessary for success in the world. We need to understand our roles, our community, and how we learn best. We need to learn what our emotions are, how to work with them, and how to build (and repair) relationships with others. We need an understanding of our strengths and weaknesses and how we can best utilize them. We took on the topic of identity at UP Academy during the second trimester of 2020. We found ourselves asking, How do you teach a five-year-old about identity? How is that different from how you teach an eight-year-old? Can you even teach someone about their identity?

The project was different for each grade level. The lower grades worked on a project titled "measure me." The major concepts were representation, communication, and identity; the smaller concepts were compare/contrast, measurement, description, cooperation, attributes, and information. The driving question was "How does my identity fit into a community?" Using games, videos, art, and activities, the educator facilitated students' exploration of roles, community, race, and genetics. The final deliverable was a life-size, accurately skin-colored depiction of themselves, wearing their favorite outfit or a dream outfit. Students measured parts of their body and re-created them on paper, cut them out, and put them together, creating a me-puzzle. Students mixed paint to match their skin tone, colored in their eyes, created hair, and dressed their paper-me.

Some students wore unicorn dresses; others wore T-shirts and shorts. My son decided on his Santa pumpkin Halloween costume, a jack-o-lantern costume with a Santa hat. Students also explored their family history and beliefs and wrote poems about themselves and their roles. They discovered their identity in the world around them.

As an educator, you can quickly see which standards are being covered through the description, activities, and concepts presented. This project covered fine motor skills, measurement in math, creativity and color mixing in art, and roles in the world as citizenship. The work comes when we ask ourselves if the lessons we teach are really what we want or need students to learn.

Crafting a concept lesson is challenging work. It requires a deep look into the values of the school and the curriculum and then ensuring they align with the lessons. Concepts need to be taught fluently in a lesson and also align with the mission, values, and guideposts of the school and community. This approach goes deeper than facts and knowledge. Concept teaching works to create a greater foundation of understanding that can be recalled and utilized during different events and lessons later in life. Students who have a deep understanding of the concepts behind lessons can transfer them and use them in all aspects of life.

This project went above and beyond the standards. It incorporated math, science, English language arts, art, creativity, problem-solving, collaboration, and critical thinking, while being engaging and fun. It challenged students to use a well-rounded thought process to look at a question and come up with their own unique answer. As our world shifts from a factory model of business to the gig economy, students need to know how to solve problems in their own unique ways, and they need to have the strength, courage, and self-assurance that their ideas are good ones.

ELEMENTARY SCHOOL IS THE FOUNDATION

Elementary school is a time in students' lives when we as educators have the opportunity to build little people. Our goal is to build them so strong that the world can't knock them down and so self-assured that they actively work to change the world around them. This is when we lay the foundation for learning for the rest of their lives.

If we think of education as a pyramid, elementary school is the large base of schooling. The pyramid gets smaller as students choose classes and specialties in middle and high school and a major or path of study in college or a masters program. Students need that broad base to balance on and support them as they continue their journey through life. That is the magic of elementary school: we get to build the foundation. As educators, we give them as many opportunities and introduce them to as many subjects, projects, ideas, and concepts as possible. This allows our learners to discern what path they want to take.

It is not our job to "track" them into roles where we think they fit, but rather to help them discover where they fit and give them the tools necessary to get there. Like the famous quote by American Activist and Founder of Children's Defense Fund, Marian Wright Edelman, "You can't be what you can't see." As we educate our youth, it is our responsibility to help them to see as many options and possibilities as we can.

THE SKILLS

The skills we need to build are often discussed and published, and they can be found in the United Nations Sustainable Development Goals. Goal #4 is to ensure inclusive and equitable quality education and promote lifelong learning opportunities for all. These goals are behind the Common Core. They are known as the Four Cs of 21st Century Skills: communication, collaboration, critical thinking, and creativity.

The Partnership for 21st Century Skills brought together experts and executives from over thirty-five major corporations. They agreed that the skills listed below are the life and career skills the workforce needs for jobs we don't even know will exist yet:

- Flexibility & Adaptability
- Initiative & Self-Direction
- Social & Cross-Cultural Skills
- Productivity & Accountability
- Leadership & Responsibility

We can teach these skills within the framework of standards. The concepts and knowledge we need to teach are also found within these frameworks. Common Core, NGSS, and other state and accepted standards are full of the content that educators are supposed to teach. How educators choose to teach it makes a great difference in the lives and mindsets of students.

For example, if we look at the California Common Core standard 2.5 for second grade social studies, we are supposed to teach *Biographies of People Who Made a Difference*. The standard asks, "Who are some people who have made a difference in our lives?" A traditional approach might be to look to the standard to see which historical figures are listed (scientists George Washington Carver, Marie Sklodowska Curie, Albert Einstein, Louis Pasteur, Jonas Salk, Charles Drew, and Thomas Edison; athletes such as Jackie Robinson and Wilma Rudolph; humanitarians like Clara Barton, Jane Addams, Henri Dunant, and Florence Nightingale; as well as authors, musicians, and artists). We could purchase posters of several of these figures to hang around the room, teach a few facts about each person, and read books about their impact on society. In a traditional approach, a teacher might assign each student a figure to write a report about, and the students would learn informational writing along with a little history. Maybe the students would be tested on which person made which difference in the world.

If we dig a little deeper, we can ask what the important concepts are surrounding the biographies of people who made a difference. We might learn how to identify a biography and how it differs from an autobiography or fiction. We could seek to understand how each person effected change amid the historical context of their lives.

We might draw a parallel between a person in history who made a difference and think that we can make a difference, too. Once we have a grasp on the concept we want to teach, we can create a project around that idea.

At UP Academy's mixed-age school, we taught this lesson as a full school theme with an overarching question: "How can I be a changemaker in my world?" We decided to help students understand how others had made change in the world and ways that they could make a difference, too.

In a mixed-age school, it is important that students have conceptual knowledge of the standards necessary for success, but when in their schooling they attain this knowledge is less important—meaning, a second grade standard doesn't need to be taught in second grade. Our upper- and lower-grade classes attacked the problem with different levels of agency, deliverables, and expectations.

Both classes started learning about changemakers and the differences they made in the world. They talked about various movements throughout history including suffrage, civil rights, gender equality, Black Lives Matter, and the 2020 election. Guest speakers who worked with refugees and are activists in the disability and Black communities shared their stories and experiences. They took a field trip to look at local murals that depict local challenges as well as national and international events and movements. Students chose a cause to march for and staged a protest march to City Hall, where the younger students gave speeches about their causes. The students worked together to design and paint a mural for change that is now in front of our school.

The upper class chose individual leaders from history to focus on. Their choices ranged from Abraham Lincoln to Kamala Harris; they researched, wrote a story board, and created backdrops and a stop-motion claymation short film about their person and the change they made in history. They also wrote to local, state, or national government representatives about a change they wished to see in the world. This project incorporated research, story-board and letter writing, informational writing, historical understanding, and art and media.

The lower class voted and decided on two different causes to focus on: Black Lives Matter and climate change. Each student joined a group, and each group learned about their challenge and created posters to share this information with others. The students wrote speeches and gave them at City Hall as well as to families on Exhibition Day, a showcase of student learning and projects for families and friends at the end of each project session. They gained a deep understanding of a few of the challenges in the world today as well as understanding some ways that they, as five-, six-, and seven-year-olds and citizens of the world, could work to make change.

THE CONCEPTS

Educators H. Lynn Erickson, Lois A. Lanning, Rachel French, and Tania Lattanzio (among others) have written books that outline in-depth concept-based learning and provide a framework for its understanding and utilization. I prefer to integrate it into all learning and especially project-based learning. Focusing on the concepts around the information we teach gives students a deeper and broader understanding of the subject material.

In our example of Social Studies Standard 2.5, we could have taught students facts about several historical figures and showed pictures of marches. But creating a claymation of a historical figure and feeling the butterflies of anticipation and the surge of pride of marching for a cause you believe in are experiences that create memories and hold deeper understanding.

When we alter the physical state of students, they learn better. The neuroscience of learning has proven that our brains retain information when there is discord between what we think we know and what the educator is saying, or when we change the physical state of the student. When students feel something, they connect with the content. Students still learn and gain an understanding of history, but we can help them do it in a way that transfers the concepts to other issues and areas of learning. That way, the learning is deeper and richer.

WHICH PHILOSOPHY IS BEST?

Each system or methodology looks at education through its own lens. Montessori believes in student agency and student-directed learning; Waldorf believes in group learning, developmentally appropriate learning, and combining hand work with academic work. The Reggio method is focused on creativity and self-expression through the learning system. New methodologies are cropping up as well—Khan Lab School (based on Khan Academy) has created their own system of project learning and independence levels. Students don't pass through grades; instead, they reach a new level of independence in their learning. These are only a few examples. Countless schools around the country are creating new methods. Even countries are continually changing their education systems. Finland just announced what they call Phenomenon-based Learning as a national educational movement. To keep up with the changing world, educational systems need to continue to change and evolve.

Many of our public and charter schools in the United States are doing things the way they have always been done. Few districts are ready or willing to put the time and expense toward creating real change in education. Some magnet and charter schools are starting to push the envelope, but they have limitations; they are still bound by the state and national regulations regarding schools and curriculum, seat time, and standardized tests. That may take a drastic turn after this global pandemic. Charters are also, generally, not innovative or accommodating when it comes to students with disabilities and tend to have fewer services available. Most private schools are guilty of this as well; even schools that serve students with disabilities often focus on one need. It takes a unique school to offer a solid base of education for all students in ways that allow students to easily transfer their knowledge, skills, and concepts to everyday life.

THE GOAL OF TEACHING

The real goal of education is to build little humans who are capable and independent, who can function productively in the world. The goal is to help students move into the real world and be able to depend on themselves and rely on their own ideas.

Recently, stories have circulated about college students' parents negotiating with professors for better grades and parents calling the bosses at their children's first jobs to make excuses for their children's mishaps. These parents' actions only hinder students' independence and confidence. These students need to learn to have difficult conversations and the limitations of self-direction. The University of California at Berkeley even offers an Adulting course for students who have no idea how to take care of themselves in the world. As educators, in tandem with parents, our job is to ensure that our students have the self-reliance, grit, and skills to be successful as they navigate a changing world.

We teach concepts, deeper learning experiences that will transfer to other areas of life beyond the school walls. We teach skills, abilities that relate to aspects of the world to increase our students' capabilities in uncertain circumstances. We teach knowledge so they can navigate conversations, understand nuances, and have a sense of their place in the world. We teach so students can effectively communicate with those around them. We teach in groups of differing abilities, race, culture, and language so students gain a global perspective of the world and can create and live with empathetic action. We teach so students can live their best lives.

WHAT IS YOUR BEST MOMENT TEACHING?

"

I can't pinpoint one, but I will say most of my memorable moments had nothing to do with curriculum or academics at all and everything to do with knowing I had made a difference for a student whether in the moment or years later when they reached out to tell me.

"

—A sixteen-year veteran educator

CHAPTER 7

MOVE FROM "GOOD STUDENT" TO "GOOD LEARNER"

THE SQUEAKY WHEEL

Liam was bright; his striking green eyes and freckled face were inquisitive, but reserved.[5] His curly mop of hair was almost always still. He was a patient listener. His parents were concerned that because he was quiet, his teacher might not notice if he fell behind. The squeaky

---

5   Name changed to protect the privacy of this student.

wheel gets the grease, as the adage goes. Liam was not a squeaky wheel. But he needed help. He was slowly falling behind. His unfinished work went unnoticed because he was a good kid. He didn't raise his hand to ask questions; he just sat silently, not understanding the work. I'm sure you've had students like Liam. In a large class, it's hard to focus on a good student who never causes problems when there are so many other issues to focus on. But in most of the United States, our large class sizes are a real disservice to students. Teachers don't have the time or bandwidth to get to know each student's learning styles and needs. And students like Liam get passed along, their confidence dwindling with the knowledge that they are not keeping up or understanding like the other students. In Liam's case, he knew he wasn't keeping up, but no one was stopping to help him.

When Liam started at UP Academy, he struggled with independent writing because he didn't know what to write about in his journal. He didn't have agency and hadn't had the freedom to just write. He didn't excel in reading, not because he couldn't read, but because he didn't have the confidence to believe he could. Others in his class were better readers, so he thought he wasn't good enough. No one had explained to him that we all learn at different paces, and it's okay. Kids are like popcorn; just because they all go in the pan at the same time doesn't mean they all pop at the same time. It's okay to not read as fast or to be better (or not as strong) in math. It's okay to learn at your own pace. Liam hadn't learned the power of "yet." He couldn't read easily—*yet*. So he felt not good enough or smart enough and not worthy of help. As a seven-year-old, he hadn't learned how to ask and advocate for his needs.

With Liam, project-based learning, community building around growth mindset, and learning about our own zones of regulation helped him grow in confidence and ability. Participation in these lessons helped Liam. He became a prolific writer and asked curiosity-driven and thought-provoking questions in class. Instead of becoming discouraged when something became difficult, he sought help and tried his best. When students understand that we are all human and no two humans are alike, when they understand that we all learn at our own pace, when they can bring a growth mindset and receive extra attention in a smaller classroom, amazing things can happen. Liam bloomed like a flower in spring.

Let's talk about how we can shift the people in our classrooms from *students*, who might sit silently when they need help, to *learners*, who take agency of their learning and advocate for their needs. Shifting this dynamic requires changes in five key areas: language, trusting students, combining concepts with experiences, environment, and influencing action.

HOW WE TALK

As educators, how we use language is extraordinarily important. When we begin to define students by their challenges, deficits, or disabilities, it not only places them in a "track" in school, but also creates an expectation gap. It establishes preconceived ideas about what that student may be capable of. Just as we can use language to lift up a student and help them see possibilities, we can also use language to unknowingly limit a student in possibilities or growth. A gentle shift occurs when, instead of saying, "Johnny can't read and it's the beginning of first grade," we say instead, "Johnny is a creative student who enjoys exploring his environment and has emerging decoding and reading skills," it changes the perception of that student for others and ourselves. We shift from expecting Johnny to be bound for failure and instead expect him to be bound for success.

It's important to talk with students in the same way. After not being in a classroom since my own elementary experience, I quickly noticed how teachers who are student centered put their students first in their minds. Instead of using terms like "kids, students, guys, children, or class" to address students, educators who focus on building confidence and creating a growth mindset will address their class as "engineers" if they are building a device for a science project, or "artists" if they are working on an art project, or (my favorite) "dendrologists" when they are working on a project about trees. It is empowering for a kindergartener to think of themselves as a dendrologist. Most of their parents don't know the word, so they get to feel important and intelligent while explaining it. They feel empowered to make scientific observations because they are dendrologists, not kindergarteners.

BUILDING TRUST

To make our lesson plans and projects more relevant and engaging, we must put our trust in our students. All of our students are capable learners, and when we truly see them as such and listen to their suggestions, ideas, and interests, we can begin our best teaching. An old quote in parenting goes "Don't worry that your children aren't listening to you, worry that they hear everything you say." We need to be congruent in our thoughts and actions with our students. We need to verbalize that we trust and respect them, and create opportunities for them to lead their own learning and model that we are listening.

When we follow students' interests and ideas and students begin to believe their ideas are important to others, they gain self-confidence. They become aware of their unique innovation and creativity. Each student will approach a problem in a manner as individual as they are. They will understand that their ideas have value and should be shared with the world. Part of our work is to teach them how to do this so their voices are heard. We work to draw out each student's strengths to build the leaders of tomorrow. We can't do that if we insist on teaching what we want them to know from a platform in front of the room. We can only do that if we come down from the pedestal, roll up our sleeves, and work alongside our students to help them discover themselves. Our work as educators is to help each of them find their light of leadership and build the skills and confidence for them to use it.

One of the best project examples of listening to students, building student trust, following student interest, and allowing for creativity is from the classroom of Heather Stinnet, a founding educator at Khan Lab School in Mountain View, California.

To cover the standards, Heather's second and third grade classes needed to do a unit on government; to work within the school's lens for that term, she needed to utilize the concept of family. She began the project by leading learning around different government structures. She facilitated discussions about what different structures meant for the people who lived under those styles. She worked with her class to decide what their deliverable would be. How would her class share their knowledge of government systems at the next Exhibition Day? Using the lens of family given to them by the school, the class decided to create a dramatic presentation of what family dinner would look like if you were a government. Here's an idea of what that looked like in a drama production. In the dictatorship, one person decided what everyone would eat, where they would sit, and what time they would eat. In contrast, in the democracy, each family member had a vote on what they would eat and free choice on where they sat. In the anarchy depiction, each member ate whatever they wanted, sat wherever they wanted (including under the table), and didn't feel any responsibility to clean up. To clarify, the dramatizations didn't show what a family who lived within that type of government might behave like; they showed how the family would behave if they were the government. It was incredibly creative and developed entirely by the students. This type of involvement in learning will ensure that they will remember how the different types of governments run and interact as they relate it back to their family dinners. They will be able to create inferences and build an understanding of global politics. You can see the chart they created as an outline of their final deliverable on the following page.

CONCEPTS AND EXPERIENCES

When we combine concepts with experiences, we offer the experience of deeper learning. In a more traditional setting, we might deliver content and explain the concept that drove the content and how it interacted with other content in the world or on a timeline. For students to have a deeper understanding, we need to add experiences to the concepts. When we do, we give students the opportunity to look at the world more broadly and understand the many different ways to approach any problem. Students who work collaboratively with others of different backgrounds and abilities gain a broader perspective of the world. They learn to see problems from multiple points of view.

Take a moment and think about this in your own life. Have you traveled to a place where you didn't speak the language? How did you solve problems when they

Basic Value to Highlight	Fairness	Self-Interest	Legacy	Authority	Ultimate Freedom
Greeting	Hello, casual, everyone says hello to everyone else, Mom and Dad	Parents greet each other, kids greet parents, Sir and Ma'am	Mother and father first, then greet in birth order, called Mother and Father	Only dictator greets everyone, then with *permission* others can speak, call parents Sir and Ma'am	They don't bother to greet each other, kids call parents by their first names or whatever they want
Who made dinner	Everyone made dinner together	Oligarch's choice	Nanny made dinner	Kid who was in trouble	Nobody
What's for dinner	Something everyone likes, or at least a few choices for everyone	Parents' favorite foods, kids have to eat it even if they don't like it	King's favorite foods	Dictator's favorite food, but leftovers for everyone else	Whatever they grab from the kitchen (donuts, candy, chips)
Kid doesn't want vegetables	Don't have to eat it	Eat it or get nothing	Have to eat it because this is what we eat!	*Must* eat it because dictator said so	He can throw it in someone's face
Consequence for no vegetables	It's okay—we'll have another one that you like another night	Totally grounded (can't go out, no electronics)	No video games for a week	Super grounded, have to make delicious dinner for others for two weeks but can only eat oatmeal themselves	No consequence
What to do this weekend	Vote on what to do	Mom and Dad's choice, kids don't get to choose but have to go.	Father's choice of doing the traditional weekend feast	Chores all day (clean the dictator's car, bathroom, etc)	Whatever they want, everyone does different things
Student school performance	Parents are interested, involved, helpful	Parents aren't interested but expect high performance	Parents expect kids to do what they did	Parents demand children be the best	Parents don't care, kids don't care
Where they sit	Circle table, equal chairs	Rectangle, kids on sides and parents on the head and foot of table	Rectangle table. King and Queen sit higher	Rectangle table, dictator at the head and the oldest kid next to dictator, others just nearby	Wherever they want (on the table, under the table, dancing next to the table, etc.)
Wrap-up	Group hug	Have to be excused to do the dishes	Say formal goodbye	Ask to be excused, say one good thing about the dictator	Just leave
Who does the dishes	All together	Kids (parents go watch TV)	Kids	Everyone except dictator	No one, they're all over the place

Remember! Values determine behavior. Families and governments are organized around their values.

arose? How did you learn to communicate, navigate, and have your needs met? If you haven't faced that particular problem, maybe you have children and you have tried to navigate a store with a stroller, or worse yet, a double stroller. Think of the solutions you needed to create to navigate that space. When students work through scenarios like these in school by taking a foreign language or working with a peer who has different mobility than they do, they learn these problem-solving skills in real time. The experience reinforces the concept.

Schools do this with field trips. Some innovative schools take learning almost entirely to the environment and use the school to cover and deconstruct knowledge they have learned in the field. At some schools in Alaska, for example, high school students build fisheries to support their towns. In the Northwest, some schools plant a tree and follow it through the growth and seasonal cycles of change to learn about habitats, ecosystems, and sustainability. Imagine planting a tree as a kindergartener and being able to study its growth through the seasons and years as you grow through elementary school, possibly even high school and college. These students develop a real and solid understanding of the life cycle, how long sustainable farming takes, and the ecosystem and patterns of growth that affect our planet.

When we create ways for students to experience our lessons and discuss the concepts in the classroom, learning becomes real. It has tangible meaning. Magic happens when we let students experience first and we explain later. If you are brave, try this in the classroom. Usually we explain how everything works, hand out materials, and lead students through the way to create the desired outcome. Instead, try giving your students the materials first and let them tinker and build however they want. Then explain the desired result and see how quickly they can get there with their materials. They will have already learned so much about what they can do that they will be able to solve the problem quickly. This flipped process allows them to invent, discover, prototype, try, fail, and try again until they get the answer. By using an experience, you are teaching them to have a growth mindset. You are teaching that failure is alright. You are giving them the freedom to discover and to learn.

When students tinker first, they learn considerably more through the process than they would by building what we tell them to. We want them to understand the learning journey, not just a predetermined desired outcome. We focus on the process, not the product. When students build what they are told, they follow directions and do what their teacher wants. When students learn by tinkering and exploring, they use their minds to think of creative solutions and work to understand the materials they are given. Educators often don't like this approach because it is messy and time consuming, and many students will not get to the desired outcome. In that mess is the crux of where learning takes place. Students become invested in their work and investigation. They try and perhaps fail, and they are ready to see how it works. They learn, listen, become engaged, and try again. This is messy, but learning, and life, are messy. It is often from the biggest messes that we learn the best lessons.

LEARNING ENVIRONMENT

When we talk about the learning environment, we can think about the physical space and ways to make it accessible and inviting to learning. We can remember the teacher who used clothespins in Dr. Sheckley's story from chapter 2. We can add flexible seating or allow students to learn in different areas of the building or classroom. We can allow students to use different modalities to learn—books, partners, computers, imagination. It can also mean setting the space, shaping the culture of the classroom, building expectations, and creating a place where all students feel safe to explore.

It's more than our physical environment, which is important. But so is the emotional environment we set up for students to feel safe, heard, and free to advocate for their needs. As educators, we do this by creating classroom agreements, promoting a growth mindset, and building a shared understanding of classroom values. This provides students with a predictable framework that creates an environment where they know they are safe to be inquisitive, curious, and helpful.

Most of the educators I have encountered create classroom agreements at the beginning of the year. This is the class code of conduct, the class set of expectations. It generally includes values like respect, kindness, and participation. Each classroom's norms are set by the educator and should be in line with the school's norms and values.

Our school agreements at UP Academy are:

- Be Kind
- Be Respectful
- Participate
- Always Do Your Best
- Have Fun Learning

Our educators then build their classroom agreements and values in line with those school agreements.

At UP Academy, Miss Brittany's class has five core values that students are expected to learn and practice each day. They get a color from the rainbow when they actively show one of her values, which are compassion, creativity, craftsmanship, curiosity, and community. In this way, students know the expectations for behavior, both from themselves and others. They have a built-in recognition system, earning the whole rainbow. They can move seamlessly to learning because their learning environment feels safe and predictable.

INFLUENCING ACTION

For education to be most impactful, students need to know how to use their learning in the world around them. This was my biggest issue as a student: what I learned never seemed to align with what mattered in the world. As educators, we can answer that challenge when we create projects that influence action in the world. We can help our students see the bridge between what they learn in school and what they do in life. We can help them see how the lessons, projects, and concepts we facilitate are useful in the real world.

One influencing action project we did at UP Academy involved Harold the dog. Harold, a therapy dog at UP Academy, has paralyzed back legs. He uses a bag to protect his legs and feet as he drags them behind him. He uses a little doggie set of wheels, like a doggie wheelchair, to go for walks and play outdoors. For this project, our elementary school partnered with the Mountain View High School Capstone Engineering Class, led by Lydia Conoway. These high school students wanted to create a device that would serve and support disabled pets. Their vision was to create and build this device and then establish a website with the dimensions and directions so anyone, anywhere could build their own device for their disabled pet. We had a pet with disabilities and a group of students who wanted to help; it was a perfect partnership. The two groups of students began by brainstorming what Harold needed and how his wheelchair could be better. His wheels were too wide, so he ran into things. They were too tall, so he got stuck on things. The wheelchair tipped over easily, and he couldn't lie down in it. Most importantly, the students needed to be able to pet him while he was in his new device.

The elementary students went to their STEAM lab to create prototypes to solve these issues. Some students worked alone, and some worked in pairs to create a vision of what they thought would work best for Harold. When the groups met again, the high schoolers took measurements of Harold, and the elementary students gave presentations of their ideas to the engineering class. The engineering class then took the ideas from the prototypes and began developing working prototypes in their lab.

We took a field trip to the high school to tour the lab, try out the new working prototypes, and give feedback. The engineering students had created feedback forms for the elementary students to share what they liked, what they didn't like, and what they thought could change to make each prototype better. Our students also got to choose which prototype they thought would work the best and explain why that was their choice. While touring the lab, the elementary students got to see the shop and the tools available to build with. They saw the laser cutter, the drill press, the 3D printers, and the power tools, and they got a better understanding of what engineering and creating looks like in practice. The engineering students took all the feedback and created a final device for Harold, which was featured on the ABC7 Bay Area News and shared on the website the students created. They have since been contacted by other families with dogs with disabilities and built another device for a dog named Fred, from Arizona, who was injured in a car accident.

While this project was about influencing action, it was also about creating experiences and opening doors of understanding. As I mentioned earlier, it is said that we cannot become what we don't see. This field trip gave students a chance to see something new. Whenever we can help our students see something new, we create a new door of opportunity for them. We never know what will leave an impression, which is why it is so important to give as many opportunities as possible.

Having experiences where students' ideas and input are used in real-world projects allows them to have a better understanding of the impact they can make in the world. It gives them confidence in their ideas and encourages them to try new things. By seeing an engineering lab, students can become inspired to create their own projects. Getting students involved in projects that make a difference in the real world lets them experience what they can become and the impact they can make on the world. If they begin to make an impact at age five, imagine what they will do at age twenty-five, or fifty!

WHAT IS THE BEST PART ABOUT BEING A TEACHER?

"

The teachable moment. When we do creative hands-on learning and the kids say this is the best day ever.

"

—Andrea Perfetti, thirty-plus-year veteran teacher

CHAPTER 8

EDUCATING YOUR PARENTS

WHY TO NOT DO IT THE WAY IT HAS ALWAYS BEEN DONE

One of the biggest unexpected challenges of starting a school has been educating the parents. I'm not sure why this was a surprise to me. I was a parent in a progressive public school, and I went through the training, too. I had to understand the benefits and how this method was different from traditional teaching. It made sense to me. The top question we get asked by prospective parents at

UP Academy is if our school will set students up with the knowledge they need for middle school. We tell them that teaching in this new way covers the same knowledge, but adds so much more. It's like getting a beautiful, colorful Cobb salad of learning instead of a bland bowl of lettuce. It adds the skills, presentations, and experiences of learning. Educating our students' parents goes far beyond marketing and into why teaching with innovative and real-life applications is valuable. We teach our parents about project-based learning, inclusive learning, and the benefits of working with hands-on materials. We show them the outcomes through exhibition days and parent conferences. They see it every day as their kids come home happy and excited about another day of doing new things.

Many of us grew up in schools where we were expected to sit in one place, face forward, pay attention, learn what was being taught, and share it back on a quiz or test. Our desks were aligned in rows and columns. In my childhood elementary school, we were seated alphabetically. When we move away from that style of learning, we also have to educate our parents and community on why we are doing the new(er) things. It is easy enough to say the old or traditional way was built on a different schedule with different needs for a different time. Now, we must educate students for the future. No one knows exactly what the future holds, but we do our best and guess what students will need. We give kids the skills to make good decisions, the experiences to understand their actions, and the knowledge we hope they'll use in future endeavors. Then, when students are self-confident, self-aware, and excited to tackle learning, they will succeed in middle school and anywhere. We don't need standardized tests to tell us if students are learning; we can watch the students instead.

Another common question we hear from parents about this more experiential, project-based learning style is what if their student falls behind (or above) grade level? This is on the minds of many parents whose children were out of school for months during the pandemic. I like to return the question and ask, "What does grade level mean, anyway?" Grade level and the standards we measure kids against were created in a government meeting room somewhere. It was an experiment to try and ensure that all kids were getting the same education, an attempt at equity and measuring attainment. Students are humans; they are dynamic and different. They each have a different brain, way of learning, and level of understanding. This is true across all subjects. If we look at any single-age classroom, there will be students reading one to two grades below level and students reading above grade level. There will be students ready for the next level of math and those struggling with the last lesson. And these might be the same students. The student who is gifted in literacy may struggle in math. The exact grade level student is like a unicorn in education. We all talk about it, but it doesn't exist. The more appropriate question is "How does the school teach to each child's level?" As educators, how we recognize and provide the just-right level of challenge in each subject for each student really is the art of teaching. When we find that sweet spot of comfort and struggle, when we are able to see students work, gain understanding, and learn, those are the lightbulb moments we live for.

In an attempt to measure grade level performance and equalize education for all, our education system developed a method to test all students. It has not improved the system; rather, it has succeeded in showing us the inequity of the public education system in the United States. It clearly defines which schools are in good neighborhoods with high income taxes that support schools and which schools and students are struggling from lower budgets and resources. Is it equitable when all kids get the same thing, or is it equitable when all kids get what they need to be successful and reach their potential?

There is a series of two images that depicts the answer to this question. It shows three children looking onto a baseball field. In the "Equality" image, all three each have a box to stand on and the tallest can see way over the fence, but the shortest is still too little to see over. The message is that they all got the same thing, so it is equal and fair. In the second image, "Equity," they each get what they need to see over the fence: the tallest doesn't need a box, but the littlest gets two boxes. In both scenarios, three boxes are used. In our classrooms, when we provide equity, everyone has an opportunity to improve. I have a friend who suggests we don't see equity until all three children are past the fence and on the baseball field. The question becomes "How can we, as educators, provide the experiences needed for our students to all succeed, at their own pace, at their own level, and feeling confident in their learning?" It doesn't help to compare students to each other. Each student is unique. When we can give them each what they need to succeed, our whole society improves.

When we look at grade level and compare our schools to those around the world, are kindergarten students in Finland at American grade level? In Finland, they don't teach reading in kindergarten. What about students who go to Waldorf schools, where they don't teach reading until age seven? Or Reggio schools, where creativity is prioritized over and along with academics? Or international schools? Students with educations that are alternatives to most American public schools often excel in high school and in the world beyond. Were they at "grade level" at every grade level? Probably not, according to our system of standards.

The question is "Does grade level matter?" It is a system made up by adults, many of whom are not in education. They wanted a way to quickly and easily assess where a grade or age group was on a certain scale of learning. The problem is, these tests measure the wrong information. What the tests really measure is the student's ability to take a test and the amount of information they can spit back up at a given moment in time. And that's the best case; the test also measures their vocabulary, what they have been exposed to at this point in their life, and how well they do under pressure. These tests can be seen as inequitable, furthering racial and economic inequities, especially when the results are tied to funding.

When we take away the notion of grade level, we can look at what is important in school. We can measure learning by progress, interest, relevance, and excitement. Educators know the importance of curiosity, creativity, and communication. What sets our students up for the best chance of success is that our students love to learn. Standardized tests don't test any of these skills. As a system, when we ask educators to teach to the test, we aren't teaching any of these skills either.

Parents will still wonder how project-based learning affects their children's grades and chances of getting into college. What matters most is that we have happy, engaged, and mentally healthy students making progress on their goals and learning every day. We have to ensure that parents understand how engaging their students will lead to this outcome.

ASSUMED COMPETENCE IN INCLUSION

Parents of students with physical disabilities are often told to believe that their student will learn less and more slowly than their peers. I want to be clear here—every child is different, every brain is different, and every brain injury is different. Students with physical disabilities often have a brain injury, so this does not ring true for every student at every moment. Nothing does. That's the point: every brain is different. But students with physical disabilities may learn just as quickly and be just as bright as their peers. We need to give them a real opportunity in an inclusive setting. When we teach in a way that encourages all students' interests and strengths, all students make progress.

Parents of students with disabilities are often really struggling. It's likely they have frequently been told all the things their child can't or won't do, and they have many times taken the advice and services that have been given to them. These parents may not have been told that their child is smart, that they can learn and deserve the opportunity to prove themself a capable and collaborative part of a class. As educators, we need to spend our time asking about student interests and strengths, not abilities. We need to understand how to fit everyone into the curriculum so that everyone can benefit. For many, this will feel uncomfortable, and teachers will need support and development around how to work with different students. It is alright to ask for help, to feel uncomfortable. In fact, it's one of the ways we know we are learning, growing, and doing the right thing.

Parents of students without disabilities often understand this idea of full inclusion faster and are willing to integrate students in a classroom. They love the idea of students learning and working together. Parents of students with disabilities often have fear surrounding how their student will fit in. They don't want their child to be made fun of or excluded. They can have a hard time seeing how it can work. But, in my experience, kids just see kids. If you give students of different abilities a way to play and work together, they will do just that.

When we presume competence and give students a chance and learn their strengths and interests, they will live up to the expectations and challenges presented to them. As educators, it is our duty to give all students this opportunity.

MARCH AWAY FROM SCREENS

In March 2020, just before the pandemic really hit America, or before we started reacting to it, our school was trying an experiment. We called it March Away from Screens. The idea was that students wouldn't use technology at home, after school, or on weekends. They were challenged to have no tech use outside of school, and in school, we used it sparingly. We found in a short amount of time that the students' methods of play, conversations, and the games they played together changed. But the road to get there wasn't easy.

When we announced the program to students, the reactions ranged from a shrug to full out crying on and off for the rest of the day. The idea of not having an iPad to go home to was terrifying and upsetting. Given this reaction from the students, I wasn't sure what to expect from the parents. We held a family meeting in the evening to share the program, the goals, the reasoning, and the prizes. Families had a discussion that ranged from "We don't use technology anyway" to "What will they do after school, how will they be engaged?" We realized that these parents had no frame of reference for children creating their own games, being bored, and becoming creative.

Ironically, the world had other plans for this experiment, as part way through March, all schools closed and learning went remote. (Out of superstition, we decided not to run the program in 2021, even though it would likely be beneficial given the increased screen time of many of our students due to the pandemic, distance learning, and changing household norms because of working-parent pressures.) But the diversity in the use of technology and the difference its absence made, even in a short amount of time, shouldn't go unnoticed.

Whether they were supportive or frightened of this experiment, all families did their best and were successful for the short duration. Ensuring students have screen-free creative time remains an important part of human development. Kids need to play; they need to build forts and have imaginative play. Kids need to be bored, they need to create games together, and they need physical movement to build the best brains.

BUILDING SMALL HUMANS

Students have all the same emotions as big humans. Sometimes these emotions are new feelings, and sometimes they are overpowering. As adults, we have felt most emotions before and have an idea of how to deal with them, whether we always choose the best way or not. As children, some of these emotions and situations are brand new, and as educators, a big part of what we do is enable children to navigate these new thoughts and experiences in productive and kind ways. We focus on social-emotional learning so students are taught to recognize emotions and use their words to solve problems.

It is important to give the same language and information to parents that their children are using. It makes the lessons cohesive from home to school and is easier for everyone. Conversely, when parents have their own methods of dealing with issues that differ from the social-emotional values of the school, it can create a struggle for the parent/teacher relationship but also confusion for the child. This is an important part of the process in admissions, being sure that family values align with the school values. The family and the educator are two important authority figures in a student's life. For the mental health of students, and to help them to thrive, it is important that families and educators reinforce each other's beliefs and systems, not work against each other.

THE HOUSE OF PERSEVERANCE

Perseverance or grit is another emotion that schools and parents talk about a lot. Our definition of perseverance is the amount of determination a student utilizes to work through something difficult. With the rise of helicopter parents, tiger parents, and just well-meaning parents who want to leave the house now, not in ten minutes, adults often do things for children that children can do for themselves. This leads to a lack of grit, a feeling of always needing help and never being good enough or fast enough. However, when we teach children to do things themselves and give them the time and space to use their skills, they build confidence, self-awareness, and new skills.

One story of perseverance is illustrated in an UP Academy STEAM camp project. The project for the afternoon was to build houses out of a set of materials. Students received flattened boxes of different sizes, cardboard rolls, stickers, paint, cones, craft sticks, glue, and tape. They could design and decorate their house however they wanted. In past groups, students had worked together and designed whole cities, using their stickers to represent power lines and connecting all the houses together into a small ecosystem. In this group, most of the students got started right away on their individual houses. This project was usually a favorite activity.

One girl sat in her chair and stared at her materials. She was not the youngest in the class, and she had no disabilities. She had been engaged in other activities all through the camp, and she enjoyed building things. But she just stared at her project. I asked her what was wrong. She looked at me and asked me to make her box. I told her I would be happy to demonstrate again on another box, or she could see how others were folding their boxes, but that I was not going to do it for her. I shared I had confidence that she could do it. And I walked away to let her try. A few minutes later she was still sitting in her chair, now with tears rolling down her face. When I asked her why she was so upset, she couldn't speak. She looked at her lap. She wouldn't look at me or the project. I again stated that I was sure she could do this. I told her I knew she was smart and capable and that if she just tried to get started, it would be easier than she thought. I again told her I wasn't going to do it for her, but that I would give her a little space for her feelings and then come back and check on her. A third check a little while later, and the same situation. She still hadn't touched the materials. I still refused to help her.

Then we talked through what finishing would look like, how she might use the stickers, her ideas for what the house might look like, as other homes in the class were being decorated and taking shape. She looked up, took hold of her flattened box, and on her first attempt, folded it into a box. She was so so proud of herself! For the rest of the day, she worked on folding her other boxes, creating her yard, and decorating her house. She took it home and proudly showed her parents what she had built. That pride, accomplishment, and success wouldn't have been possible if I had done it for her. I shared this story with her parents later that night. I wanted them to know her struggle and how to continue to support her journey to find her grit. When students succeed, as well as when they struggle, it is important to involve the family so they can support your efforts and their students.

Creating a safe space for learning, trying, failing, and success is key to student motivation and grit. Every good educator knows that the relationships you build with your students allow them to ask questions and grow. Focusing on the social-emotional growth of our students isn't something that is "nice to do"; it is imperative for their success in school and in life. Involving the parents in these discussions and ensuring that students receive a streamlined vision of the world around them allows for less stress for the student and the educator. Perseverance, grit, and confidence can be learned, but it requires patience and the ability to trust and allow for failure. Parents and educators need to work together to provide and support these learning opportunities.

WHAT DO YOU THINK IS THE BIGGEST CHALLENGE IN EDUCATION?

"

Changing the whole system so students' learning needs are actually met. This takes a whole mindset change on the part of lawmakers and educators.

"

—Mariaemma Willis, thirty-year veteran educator

CHAPTER 9

THE FUTURE OF EDUCATION

DISTANCE LEARNING IN 2020

Schools have changed, and continue to change at a rapid pace due to the COVID-19 pandemic. For the first time for as long as I can remember, everyone is talking about education. Educators, parents, thought leaders, and ed tech companies are all contemplating what education means. They are questioning what it is for, what we are teaching, and what we are measuring. It is an exciting time, but also one fraught with anxiety and fear. Change is never easy, and this drastic amount of change was thrust upon society when our schools were no longer safe places for students to learn and teachers to teach because of the coronavirus.

The pandemic has forced schools to find a new way to teach. Many have taken the curriculum and teaching methods used in school and are attempting to do the same online. They discipline students who don't pay attention, don't look at the camera, or don't log in for class. Other more progressive, and arguably more successful, schools are finding ways to reinvent their curriculum. They are teaching in a new, fresh, engaging way that motivates students to log in and participate. These students are excited to work and share their progress.

Schools that have created relevant projects that students could work on independently at home while logged in with a supportive educator have seen students more engaged and connected to their learning and their peers. As a parent, I struggled to get my kids to log in for math or English lessons, but after lunch they were asking if it was time to log in for project time yet. By supporting student interests and passion projects, educators could coach and facilitate learning. Students were intrinsically motivated to work toward their goals—because they chose and set their own goals. As educators, we need to understand these lessons of the pandemic and work to incorporate these learnings into our classrooms as we move back to normal. We need to work to change normal to something different than it was before.

THE FUTURE OF WORK

We must cultivate the qualities and characteristics companies will be looking for in the future. We need to understand what qualities are necessary in our future workers and leaders and teach those for the success of our students. The job of schools is ultimately to ready the next generation for the challenges they will face. The World Economic Forum (www.weforum.org) lists critical thinking, creativity, problem-solving, flexibility, resilience, and active learning as a few of the most important characteristics adults will need in the future. If we look at how many schools approach education, we can see that we aren't teaching flexibility by asking all of our students to sit still and listen. We aren't teaching critical thinking skills by feeding them information and asking them to choose the correct answer on a test. We aren't teaching them problem-solving by doing a couple of activities in class. Today's students need rich, meaningful projects that make a difference in the world. They need to understand how they fit into the world and what difference they may want to make in it.

SCHOOL AS DAYCARE

We have seen that one major component of school is the daycare aspect. Younger students are looked after for eight to ten hours per day so their adults can work. That isn't likely to change as many families with two working parents have added managing their child's schooling to their already long list of to-dos. Almost three million women left the workforce in the past year (2020–2021), potentially setting back the women's movement by decades. Families who can afford to live on one income, at least temporarily, have attempted to do so. Children need to attend schools, but shifting what they do there will make a huge impact on their individual futures and the future of our country and our planet.

THOUGHTS FROM THOUGHT LEADERS

When I have discussed education with thought leaders, educators, and students, several themes arose. We need to respect our students and our young people. We need to ask them what is important to learn and to make a difference in the world. We need to spend the time coaching, supporting, and facilitating their actions toward making a change. When we do that, everyone wins.

You may be thinking, *I teach elementary school, that's not really possible.* A lot of knowledge and skills need to be taught in elementary school to make these big changes and leaps in education possible in middle school and beyond. These students need a base of knowledge and understanding to grow upon. It is more important than ever that we teach in ways that include all students. We need to choose a curriculum that doesn't leave anyone behind. Our students should be able to learn in a hands-on, experiential, project-based way from the start. All students need to learn the three Rs: reading, writing, and arithmetic. That hasn't changed. However, we need to enhance the way we teach these skills and the way students understand they are used. Subjects are not silos; students need to read to understand word problems, and they need to write to explain their answers. Knowledge is all connected, as is every subject from physics to social sciences. When we work to help students understand these connections, when we teach in a multisensory, multifaceted, multiconnected way, we enable their transfer of knowledge into the real world. We enable the use of information to create change. That is the greatest gift we can give the next generation.

Each group of thought leaders and educators has their own way to make change. There is a lot of conversation around student-centered learning, sustainable education, education to solve the world's biggest problems, education that follows the SDGs, creating an ecosystem of learning that involves communities, and others. The common threads here are that they are listening to learners, facilitating learning, and allowing for student experiences to build skills. All of this has been covered in this book and are good aspects of project-based learning. No matter the focus of the educational pedagogy and methodology, students need to be in the center. When we put students' needs and ideas first, everyone improves.

SMALLER IS BETTER

As we make the shift to focusing on our classes, we get to know our students. As we work to create experiences for them, differentiate to their level, and personalize projects to their interests, we need to decrease class sizes. We need to create smaller schools. We have seen how large schools with a history of traditional teaching handled change during the pandemic. They were like barges in the river attempting to make a U-turn; it was slow, they got stuck, and many never made the turn. In contrast, the smaller schools were like motorboats, quickly

CONCLUSION

I hope this book has entertained, enlightened, and empowered you to think differently about education, your students, and your classroom. A revolution begins not with one person leading the way for change but instead when many people see the need for change and begin to take small stands individually and together.

We are at a moment when crisis is meeting opportunity. We have the chance to make real and lasting change in education by the ways we teach when we walk back into our classrooms. But the year 2021 is not unique in that aspect. We have the opportunity to make real and lasting change every time we set foot in our classrooms. That is why we teach—to touch the lives of students and make change in the world.

I urge you to try some of the examples explained in this book. If this is new to you, start small. Start a wonder wall in your classroom. Try a small mini-project and do some messy hands-on activities. As your comfort with a more autonomous classroom grows, try bigger, messier projects with your students. I challenge every educator who reads this book to try a full multi-subject, in-depth, long project—a project where your students get to dig into a driving question, explore the underlying concepts, and share their ideas and conclusions with an active and authentic set of stakeholders. There are ideas for these kinds of projects all over your school and community. Ask your students what they would change and start there. Involve the community and create an ecosystem of learning, and see where that takes you and your students in your learning and development.

I am also available as a resource. Our website, rebeleducator.com, offers professional development for educators and school districts as well as programs for entrepreneurs looking to start their own schools. The website has a full project library for educators and a free download of our project template to help you start planning and developing your own projects. We lead courses and are available to work with you, your team, or your school to develop a project- and concept-based culture that is student focused.

I encourage you to start creating your own experiences in your classroom. Create your own clothespin system, create your own activities, field trips, and projects. Follow your students' interests and ideas. You and your students will learn a lot in the process, and I'd love to hear about it. When you utilize the projects available on rebeleducator. com, you become a part of our community. Whether you use projects from us or ones you create, I'd love to hear how your projects take shape in your classroom.

Learning is flexible and creative, it is challenging and supportive, requirering mental strength and a growth mindset. Take the ideas presented in this book through theory and story, implement them in your classroom, and make them yours.

I invite you to be a part of the education revolution. Be a Rebel Educator.

100 percent of the proceeds of this book go to UP Academy, Inc., and support an education that resists tradition for students of all abilities.

ACKNOWLEDGMENTS

In no particular order and apologies to anyone I may have forgotten.

Barry Sheckley, Ph.D.
Susan Sheckley
Chris Sheckley
John Mathias
Susan Lin
Fredlyn Berger
Anne Marie Roberts
Jocelyn DeGance Graham
Alexandra Kelly
Brittany Botta
Freedom Cheteni
Audrey O'Donnell

Iman Guiga

Michelle Daly

Carolyn Freedman

Elizabeth Gauthier

My children and all the students and families of UP
   Academy

The almost one hundred educators who completed a
   survey to share their thoughts with me,
   including those who are quoted in the book

Alexia Vernon

Emily Gindlesparger, Frances Jane O'Steen, Bianca
   Pahl, and the Scribe team

Aimée Skidmore

Ciaara Ashlie

Mark Metry

Deborah Olatunji

Ramona Pierson

Heather Stinnett

Eleonora Tamasne

Gabriella Souza

Thom Markham, Ph.D.

Esther Wojcicki

Rebecca Westover, EdD

Bob Lenz

Kyle Wagner

Nicole Jarvis Babaoglu